The Animals in War memorial in Park Lane, London, acknowledges man's exploitation of many creatures, from elephants to pigeons and glow-worms.

Animal Graves and Memorials

Jan Toms

A Shire book

Published in 2006 by Shire Publications Ltd,
Cromwell House, Church Street, Princes Risborough,
Buckinghamshire HP27 9AA, UK.
(Website: www.shirebooks.co.uk)

Copyright © 2006 by Jan Toms.
First published 2006.
Shire Album 452. ISBN-10: 0 7478 0643 8;
ISBN-13: 978 0 7478 0643 1.
Jan Toms is hereby identified as the author of this work in
accordance with Section 77 of the Copyright, Designs and
Patents Act 1988.

British Library Cataloguing in Publication Data:
Toms, Jan
Animal graves and memorials. – (Shire album; 452)
1. Pet cemeteries – Great Britain
2. Memorials - Great Britain
I. Title 636'.0887'0941
ISBN-13: 978 0 7478 0643 1.
ISBN-10: 0 7478 0643 8.

Cover: *At Arlington Court in Devon Miss Rosalie Chichester's dog Memory rests on a pedestal that commemorates Vanguard, from a previous age.*

ACKNOWLEDGEMENTS

Photographs are acknowledged as follows: Bosworth Hall Hotel, page 44 (left); Childwick Bury Stud, page 36; Liz Cooke, back cover; Chris Cornell, page 31 (left); Linda Delandro, page 29 (both); Essex Police Museum, page 27; The Famous Grouse Distillery, page 75 (top two); Rosemary Goodall, page 85; the Home of Rest for Horses, page 10 (bottom); Michael J. Hulme (courtesy of Heather Bayne), page 8; Val Hurlston-Gardiner, pages 24 (top) (courtesy of Sir Roy Strong), 35 (top), 60 (left); Cadbury Lamb, pages 1, 4, 11, 12, 13 (bottom), 14, 16 (top right), 17, 20, 23 (bottom), 24 (bottom), 25, 28, 30, 31 (right), 32, 33 (both), 34, 35 (bottom), 41 (both), 43, 44 (right), 45 (left), 47 (both), 50, 51, 53 (top), 55, 56 (bottom), 57, 58, 59 (both), 60 (right), 62, 63 (top), 64 (top), 66 (both), 67 (top), 68, 69, 72 (bottom), 76, 78 (bottom), 79, 81, 82 (top), 83; Cadbury Lamb (courtesy of The Royal Regiment of Fusiliers), page 56 (top); Lucinda Lambton, page 13 (top); John McKenna (www.john.mckenna.com), page 74; Antony Miles Ltd (courtesy of The Royal Gloucestershire, Berkshire and Wiltshire Regiment Museum), page 72 (top); Barbara Mitchell, page 65; Newstead Abbey, page 5; Piershill Cemetery, page 75 (bottom); Sandy Pittendreigh, page 78 (top); The Potteries Museum and Art Gallery, page 63 (bottom); Becky Proctor, pages 15, 22; courtesy of RAF Scampton Museum, page 45 (right); Sue Ross, page 64 (bottom); Leslie Sklaroff, page 6; Jan Toms, pages 3, 7 (both), 9, 10 (top), 19 (all), 23 (top), 26, 37, 38, 40, 48, 49, 52, 53 (bottom); Jan Toms (courtesy of the National Trust), front cover; Sue Trueman, pages 70, 82 (bottom); Sue White, page 67.

The author is also particularly grateful to the following for their assistance: Geoff and Joy Burn, Jo Darke PMSA, Ray Doe, Graham Greasley, Bob and Jackie Hampton, Richard and Sheila Lee, Doug McAll, Doug McBeath, Colin Metcalfe, John Nettleton, David Pringle, John Ravenscroft, Patrick Roberts (www.purr-n-fur.org.uk), Charlie Scott, and Sally Williams of the London Parks and Gardens Trust.

Printed in Malta by Gutenberg Press Limited, Gudja Road, Tarxien PLA 19, Malta.

Contents

A rabbit's gravestone at the Pets at Rest cemetery, Newport, Isle of Wight.

The grave of the Olympic show-jumping champion Foxhunter on the Blorenge mountain near Abergavenny in Monmouthshire.

Introduction

'Closely bound to human heart.'
Memorial to **Jerry**, a poodle, at Wicksteed Park, Kettering

When Lord Byron buried his dog **Boatswain** at Newstead Abbey in 1808 he experienced conflicting emotions. There was grief for something loved and lost and gratitude to the dog that saved him from drowning. At the same time, in erecting a memorial of monumental proportions he demonstrated his own wealth and position. In his funerary lines 'All the virtues of man with none of his vices', Byron projected on to Boatswain unrealistic goodness yet expressed confusion and anger that an animal may be 'Denied in Heaven the Soul he held on Earth'. Had his fortunes not forced him to sell Newstead, Byron intended to be buried with his dog.

Boatswain died having been bitten by a rabid dog. In 1992 a similar fate befell Sir Roy Strong's cat **Muff**, infected with feline AIDS by a feral cat. His owners suffered 'a torrent of emotion and tears', erecting a striking edifice topped by a golden ball placed along 'Sir Muff's Parade' in their Herefordshire garden. Muff's qualities of courage and affection were fulsomely sung.

From time immemorial man has used animals for his own benefit, whether for food, transport, sport or simply companionship. Many people have found in a pet the constancy lacking in their human relationships. Sigmund Neuburger, 'the Great Lafayette', an illusionist and bachelor, adored his dog **Beauty.** She wore a jewelled collar and his car radiator sported her effigy. When she died in Edinburgh in 1911

Boatswain was Lord Byron's dog and is buried at Newstead Abbey, Nottingham-shire, under an elaborate monument.

he insisted on her burial in the human cemetery, permitted only when he reserved the grave for himself. Two weeks later he was killed, thus joining his beloved pet.

Loneliness fuels many animal–human relationships. Frederica, Duchess of York, who came to Britain from Prussia to marry the 'Grand Old Duke', surrounded herself with fifty dogs, and many of their tombstones are still visible at Oatlands in Surrey. Queen Alexandra mourned **Togo**, her dog, 'The joy and pleasure of my life', while Prince Chula Chakta-Bongse, cousin of the King of Siam, when a student at Cambridge in 1934 lost his pet **Tony** and donated a fountain in recognition of the 'friendship and happiness' the dog provided.

In turn, dogs have shown remarkable loyalty to their dead masters. Most famous is **Greyfriars Bobby**, a Skye terrier who stayed at his master's graveside in Edinburgh for fourteen years, sleeping there in all weathers and defying attempts to re-home him. The Provost of Edinburgh paid for his dog licence and when Bobby died a plaque was erected with the words 'Let his loyalty be a lesson to us all'. In similar vein, a sheepdog named **Tip** remained with her dead master on Howden Moor in Derbyshire in 1953. She was found fifteen weeks later, not having strayed more than 25 yards from his body. A monument to her loyalty was erected at the Derwent Reservoir, paid for by public subscription. In 1805 Charles Gough died in a climbing accident and his bitch remained at his side, whelping a puppy. The incident was immortalised in two poems, 'Fidelity' by Wordsworth and 'Helvellyn' by Sir Walter Scott. Landseer painted the scene, naming the picture 'Attachment'.

The story of Greyfriars Bobby, romanticised in a film made in 2005, is commemorated in Greyfriars churchyard, Edinburgh.

Some animals have become *causes célèbres*, such as the nameless brown terrier used for prolonged experimentation at University College, London. When in 1902 Battersea Council gave permission for a statue to be erected, it became a focus for supporters and opponents of vivisection, resulting in the '**Brown Dog** riots', the biggest until the poll-tax demonstrations of the 1980s. The statue disappeared but a replacement was erected in 1985, near to the peace pagoda in Battersea Park.

There was less violent though righteous dissent over the statue of **Copenhagen**, the Duke of Wellington's charger. When the sculptor began work Copenhagen had already died, so he used as a model a mare called Rosemary. Critics complained that she bore no resemblance to the famous horse. In 1999 a similar row broke out at Sandiway in Cheshire when a new pub sign was commissioned for the **Blue Cap**, the name celebrating

The statue of 'Brown Dog' in Battersea Park, London, highlights the use of animals in scientific experiments.

a famous hunting dog that died in 1772. The depiction was likened to the cartoon dog Snoopy and had to be amended.

Where pets' 'souls' go to has shadowed many bereavements. On the death of her Pekinese **Crocus Bud**, the Marchioness of Dufferin and Ava plaintively wrote: 'Is there a country, Lord, where though dost keep a place for dogs that fall asleep?' Lady Florence Dixie of Bosworth Hall, on losing her dog **Smut** beneath the wheels of a train, wrote: 'Immortal in thy spirit, await me where... I can rejoin thee n'er to part again.' Sir Henry Newbolt composed a poem, 'Fidele's Grassy Tomb', to a dog that, like Boatswain, saved his master from drowning. The real life 'Fidele' was **Azor**, a poodle given to Thomas Swymmer Champneys by the King of Prussia in 1790 and whose remains were found in the family vault, thus fuelling the debate about permitting animals in consecrated ground. Azor's monument stands in Orchardleigh churchyard near Frome. Mrs Louise Sophie Harris was allegedly incensed when her dog **Vida** was denied a Christian burial and so she built St John's Chapel at Matlock, erecting a plaque to her pet, 'Till the Last and Brightest Easter Day be Born'.

The monument to the dog Azor, by the south door of St Mary's Church, Orchardleigh, Somerset, is unusual in standing in consecrated ground.

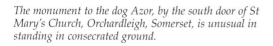

Animals having shorter life spans than humans, the death of a pet is often a child's introduction to mortality. A simple dedication to 'Goldie – God Bless our Bunny' at the Pets at Rest Cemetery, Newport, Isle of Wight, illustrates this fact (see page 3).

War can be a beastly business. In the First World War, dogs were recruited from Battersea Dogs' Home. Some 7500 died. In the Second World War the United States Army trained 10,000 dogs for military service. 200,000 pigeons were donated to the war effort between 1939 and 1945.

Rifleman Khan, an Alsatian, showed amazing selflessness in returning to the water during the bombardment at Walcheren, rescuing his handler, Jimmy Muldoon, who could not swim. After the war, a 'tug of love' developed between the original owners and Muldoon – resolved when the mutual affection between soldier and dog was witnessed. Khan was buried at Edinburgh Castle. **Rob**, a collie, showed a remarkable aptitude for parachuting. Behind enemy lines he warned his companions of enemy approach by licking them awake. A plaque was erected to his achievements in his owners' garden at Tetchill in Shropshire.

Some dogs survived wartime dangers only to die in road traffic accidents. **Hambone Junior** was a 'gingery mongrel with

Commissioned to record the life of a much decorated parachute dog, Rob, this memorial stands in a garden at Tetchill in Shropshire.

'Turpitz', a shipwrecked pig, was used as a fund raiser during the First World War and now decorates the Imperial War Museum, Lambeth, London.

black patches', the adopted mascot of the 47th Infantry Regiment of the 9th Division, US Army, stationed at Alresford in Hampshire. Hambone was run over in 1944. In 1962 the American vice-consul at Southampton unveiled a headstone to him in Ladywell Lane, Alresford. A similar fate befell **Nigger**, the Labrador of Guy Gibson, who died while his master was bombing the Eider and Mohne dams. He is buried at RAF Scampton. A bitch called **Bobbie** accompanied the 66th Berkshire Regiment to Afghanistan and was wounded in the Battle of Maiwand in 1880. She was presented to Queen Victoria but was shortly afterwards run over by a hansom cab. She is on display at the regimental museum at Salisbury. **Bob**, the Crimea dog, served with the 1st Battalion Scots Guards. He was awarded a medal for chasing cannonballs but met a sad end under the wheels of a butcher's cart. He is displayed at the National War Museum of Scotland.

Perhaps the most unusual war hero is **Turpitz,** a pig rescued following the sinking of the *Dresden*. Turpitz was brought to England as a 'prisoner of war' and regularly auctioned in aid of the Red Cross. When he died his head was mounted and his trotters turned into carving sets and these are now at the Imperial War Museum.

In contrast, **Cupid**, the pet pig of the first Countess of Mount Edgcumbe, led a pampered life, travelling everywhere with his mistress. When he died he was reputedly buried in a gold casket placed beneath a 30 foot obelisk, later moved to overlook Plymouth Sound.

During the First World War eight million horses were killed by gunfire, disease or starvation. The tender-hearted Elgar wrote: 'I walk round and round the room cursing God for allowing dumb beasts to be tortured.' In 1942 400,000 horses, mules and donkeys were sent to the Eastern Front. From Southampton, a grey gelding called **Warrior** served with the Old Contemptibles, suffering shrapnel injuries. On his return he was presented to the city, complete with a bag of sugar. When he died a memorial stone was erected at Southampton Golf Course. Another **Warrior**, owned by Colonel Jack Seely, Lord Mottistone, was, in the words of Brough Scott, 'one of the greatest horses in history'. His adoring owner wrote a book, *My Horse Warrior,* and his obituary quoted Byron's 'Denied in Heaven'.

A drinking trough at Lake on the Isle of Wight.

TO THE HORSES AND DOGS WHO ALSO BORE THE BURDEN AND HEAT OF THE DAY 1914 — 1920

The Household Cavalry horse Sefton survived the IRA bombing in Hyde Park in 1982, returned to duty and ultimately retired to the Home of Rest for Horses at Speen, Buckinghamshire. This stone is at the Defence Animal Centre, Melton Mowbray, Leicestershire.

In the Second World War **Olga, Regal** and **Upstart** received medals for courage from Maria Dickin, founder of the PDSA. More recently, **Sefton, Echo** and **Yeti** achieved recognition for their suffering in the Hyde Park bombing of 1982. Sefton suffered sixteen shrapnel wounds. His memorial is at the Defence Animal Centre at Melton Mowbray.

Faith, a cat who endured a bombing raid on the church of St Faith and St Augustine, Watling Street, in the City of London, showed exceptional courage in protecting her kitten and was awarded a 'civilian' medal. The Archbishop of Canterbury attended the ceremony and Faith was buried at the church gates.

Numerous drinking troughs were erected in memory of horses that died in war while the Peace Pledge Union donated a house in Kilburn to the RSPCA to act as a veterinary surgery in memory of animals killed in conflict. In 2004 a national monument to all animals killed in war was erected at Brook Gate, Park Lane, London.

There are numerous monuments to horses, celebrating their achievements. Edward VII erected a statue to his Derby winner **Persimmon** at Sandringham. The horse nearly missed the race, taking exception to travelling by train. **Red Rum** lies at the finishing post at Aintree while **Golden Miller, Arkle** and **Dawn Run**, all Gold Cup winners, have statues at Cheltenham racecourse.

SEFTON
A BRAVE CAVALRY HORSE
WHO SURVIVED THE BOMBING
OUTRAGE IN HYDE PARK ON
20TH JULY 1982
SERVED WITH THE HOUSEHOLD
CAVALRY MOUNTED REGIMENT
1967 - 1984
RETIRED AT THE HOME OF
REST FOR HORSES
1984 - 1993

Animal memorials wax lyrical in a way rarely indulged on human tombstones. 'A model of the truest love', ' A gentleman among dogs', 'Possessed of immortal virtues', 'Faithful as woman, braver than man', 'In whom we lost Sagacity, Love and Fidelity' – so say the accolades. Perhaps the most unusual, with a wry touch of humour, is to Hew Kennedy's **Scruffy**: 'Severe incontinence cut short a long life at the age of 18 years... If her bladder had been stronger, she would have lasted even longer.'

Gazetteer

ENGLAND

BEDFORDSHIRE

SILSOE

In 1876, after visiting her friend Lady Cowper, Lady Palmerston was heard to comment: 'How I do pity poor Anne, living alone at Wrest, surrounded by all those graves of her family.' Graves there were, sixteen in all, only they were not of relatives but of dogs. Wrest Park, a flamboyant house built in the style of a French *château*, had been home to the powerful de Grey family, Earls of Kent, since the thirteenth century. In about 1830, perhaps in response to the death of a family pet, the then Lord Grantham, second Earl de Grey, commissioned a statue of a dog in Portland stone to mark the site of a canine cemetery. He also painted the scene. The earliest burial was in that year, of **Phedra.** The last was that of **Kelpie**, buried in 1889. The original statue was replaced in the 1970s but the graves are still extant.

The house was once used as a residence for the United States Ambassador and later was occupied by the Silsoe Research Institute. The grounds are cared for by English Heritage.

Wrest Park, Silsoe, Bedfordshire MK45 4HS. English Heritage. Telephone: 01525 860152.

SOUTHILL

In 1806 Samuel Whitbread of Southill House wrote a poem in remembrance of **Jock**, his wife's spaniel. Beneath a drinking fountain, surmounted by a Coade stone

In the centre of the dogs' cemetery at Wrest Park, Silsoe, is this memorial.

sculpture of Jock modelled by Garrard, the verse called upon:

Ye dogs who in succession share
Your kindest lady's tender care
Drink at this fount, for see above
A model of the truest love.

Southill House is a private residence.

WOBURN

Chee Foo, also known as Wuzzy, was a Pekinese pet of Mary, eleventh Duchess of Bedford. When he died, the Duchess erected a Corinthian-columned temple to his memory in the 3000 acre deer sanctuary of the park at Woburn Abbey. It is visible from the visitors' road. The Duchess died in 1937 when her plane crashed as she was about to complete two hundred hours of solo flying.

Also at Woburn is a statue of **Mrs Moss**, the 'Bloomsbury Stud's famous brood mare', bought in 1975. She produced fifteen foals, including twelve winners. Of these, Jupiter Island, winner of the Japan Cup, was the first British-bred horse to run $1^1/2$ miles in 2 minutes 25 seconds. Mrs Moss died in 1991. Her statue is by Philip Blacker.

Woburn Abbey, Woburn, Bedfordshire MK17 9WA. Telephone: 01525 290333. Website: www.woburnabbey.co.uk

BERKSHIRE
WINDSOR

The Victorian royal family had a penchant for pugs. A bronze statue of **Bosco** stands in the grounds of Frogmore, where Queen Victoria and Prince Albert are buried. A statue of Bosco also stands outside Queen Victoria's bedroom at Osborne House, Isle of Wight.

Edward VII's companion, a fox terrier named **Caesar**, accompanied the king on visits abroad and, when Edward died, followed his funeral cortege, being afterwards inconsolable. Caesar was buried with an epitaph composed by Queen

A statue of Mrs Moss greets visitors on the entrance drive to Woburn Abbey.

The writer Lucinda Lambton erected an obelisk to her dog Flint in her garden at Hedgerley.

Alexandra: 'Our beloved Caesar, who was the King's faithful and constant companion until death and my greatest comforter in my loneliness and sorrow for four years after, died April 18 1914.'

Edward lies in St George's Chapel, Windsor, and after the First World War, a statue of Caesar was placed at his feet.
Windsor Castle, Berkshire. Telephone: 020 7766 7304. Website: www.royalcollection.org.uk

BUCKINGHAMSHIRE
HEDGERLEY

When Lucinda Lambton's lurcher, **Flint**, was tragically killed, she searched the country for a suitable memorial, settling appropriately upon a simple obelisk in flint, bearing his name. It stands in the garden of her Buckinghamshire home. *Private residence.*

LATIMER

At the Battle of Boshof in 1900, during the Boer War, the life of Major General Lord Chesham was gallantly saved by the French General de Villebois Mareuil, who was killed in the act. Although an enemy, Mareuil was buried with full military honours. In recognition of this act of bravery, Lord Chesham brought Mareuil's wounded horse to England. When it died on 5th February 1911, its heart and trappings were buried on the village green, next to the war memorial.

On the green at Latimer is this memorial to the horse of a French general killed during the Boer War.

The Home of Rest for Horses at Speen in Buckinghamshire housed three horses injured in the Hyde Park bombing. Visitors can read about them at the stables.

SPEEN

On 20th July 1982 two soldiers and seven horses were injured in a terrorist bomb blast in Hyde Park, London. In spite of suffering sixteen shrapnel wounds, **Sefton**, a black cavalry horse, returned to work. Regarded as a hero, on completing his service he was retired to the Home of Rest for Horses, where he died in 1993, aged thirty.

Echo, a grey police horse, was also on duty that day but, because of his injuries and the subsequent trauma, he was unable to continue working and retired to the same home. He died in December 2003, aged thirty-two. His saddle, displaying shrapnel shards and nails, along with cards received by the horses from members of the public, are in the museum at the Metropolitan Police Mounted Training Establishment at Thames Ditton, Surrey.

A third victim, **Yeti,** a black gelding, served with the Household Cavalry for four more years after the bombing and then spent eighteen years in retirement at the home, where he died in May 2004 aged thirty-six. To commemorate their lives, a picture board is on display at the visitor centre at the home.

Home of Rest for Horses, Westcroft Stables, Speen, Princes Risborough, Buckinghamshire. Telephone: 01494 488464. Website: www.homeofrestforhorses.co.uk

WADDESDON MANOR

By the path leading west from the aviary is a gravestone to **Poupon**, 'favourite pet poodle' of Baron Rothschild. The dog died in October 1902.

Waddesdon Manor, Waddesdon, near Aylesbury, Buckinghamshire HP18 0JH. Telephone: 01296 653226. Website: www.waddesdon.org.uk

CAMBRIDGESHIRE
CAMBRIDGE

Prince Chula Chakta-Bongse, cousin to the King of Siam, attended Trinity College, Cambridge. When his dog **Tony** died in 1934 he donated a dogs' drinking

A dogs' drinking fountain in Cambridge, funded by Prince Chula of Siam.

fountain to Cambridge City Council, bearing the inscription: 'In memory of Tony, a dog who gave him friendship and happiness during his Cambridge years, this trough was erected by his Royal Highness Prince Chula of Siam.' Now sadly neglected, the fountain stands next to Lloyds Bank at Mitcham Corner. A similar fountain donated by the prince is at Bodmin, Cornwall.

HORSEHEATH

Bred by the Batson family from Jamaica and trained at Horseheath Lodge, **Plenipotentiary,** winner of the 1834 Derby, is commemorated in the Horseheath village sign. He tended to be overweight and a rival jockey described how 'I saw a great bullock cantering at my side'. Later, Plenipotentiary was said to have 'carried enough blubber to sink a South Sea whale'. He was a difficult horse and his stud career was reduced to covering mares for a farmer.

MOLESWORTH

Molesworth Pet Cemetery, founded by E. Grey of Hyde Park Gate, London, began operation in 1903. More than a hundred years later, about seventy-five graves remain out of more than 250, including those of monkeys and a marmot. The owners, Geoff and Joy Burn, hold the original burial records. Among the graves is that of a dog belonging to the King of Belgium. Baron von Hugel, the traveller and philosopher, believed that as dogs stood in relation to man so man stood in relation to God, and he had his Pekinese, **Teufel** and **Puck**, buried in grave 278.

There is also a Molesworth Pet Cemetery in New Zealand.

NEWTON

The village war memorial at Newton includes a drinking trough 'Dedicated to horses killed in World War One and the South African War'.

A photograph from the 'Daily Mirror' in 1912 shows a dog burial at Molesworth Pet Cemetery. The dog on the column had been removed but was returned to the present owners.

WANDLEBURY

Romance surrounds the life of **Godolphin Arabian** (1724–53). Originally named Scham ('Wind'), he was given to Louis XV of France by the Bey of Tunis; according to folklore, he was accompanied by his mute groom, Agba, and a cat. Louis thought him valueless and Scham was reduced to pulling a water cart in Paris. Starved and beaten, he was rescued by Mr Coke, a Norfolk Quaker, and taken to England but as he recovered his strength he became unmanageable. Scham was again starved to make him controllable and, when Agba broke in to visit him, the horse's welcoming call alerted the guards. Agba was charged with trespass and committed for trial. The aunt of Lord Godolphin, hearing of the case, persuaded her nephew to intervene and horse, groom and cat were transferred to his stud at the Gog Magog Hills. When Godolphin's stallion Hobgoblin was brought to serve his mare Roxana Scham broke free and challenged the stallion, covering the mare himself. This act infuriated Godolphin but when he saw the quality of Roxana's foal he changed his mind. The Godolphin Arabian's blood still contributes to the success of the English thoroughbred. Scham lived to be twenty-nine and is buried under a slab at Wandlebury, now run by the Cambridge Preservation Society.

Cambridge Preservation Society, Wandlebury Ring, Gog Magog Hills, Babraham, Cambridge. Telephone: 01223 243830. Website: www.cpswandlebury.org

CHESHIRE
CONGLETON

Mariana Percy Lawton, mistress of Lawton Hall, lonely, estranged from her husband, mourning the death of her female lover, owned a bullfinch named **Bullie**, which she taught to sing 'God Save the Queen'. When it died in 1853 a memorial was erected. Mariana wrote:

> Then farewell my bird, I give thee this grave
> In return for the pleasure thou often me gave.
> The sun will shine o'er thee, thou are free from the storm.
> These flowers will be freshened by the tears of the morn.

The hall has fallen into neglect but Bullie's headstone will be installed in the Lawton Memorial Hall.

DUNHAM MASSEY

The first recorded animal grave at Dunham Massey, home of the Earls of Warrington, is of a Dutch mastiff known as **Pugg,** alias Old Vertue, buried in 1702. Pugg's portrait, painted by Jan Wyck, hangs in the Great Gallery. Other dog memorials include: **Poor Tipler**, 1762; **Poor Turpin**, 1783; **Poor Cato**, 1786.

Dunham Massey, Altrincham, Cheshire WA14 4SJ. National Trust. Telephone: 0161 941 1025.

One of the finely incised animal gravestones at Dunham Massey.

EATON HALL

From the mid nineteenth century horses of the Grosvenor family, Dukes of Westminster, have been commemorated at their celebrated stud. These include: **Angelica** (1879–99), **Beeswing** (1833), whose bones are at the stud, and the 1880 Derby winner, **Bend Or** (1877–1903), described by his trainer as 'the best horse in the world'. His skull is at the Natural History Museum, South Kensington. **Flying Fox** (1896–1911), also described as one of the greatest horses of all time, died in France. His skeleton is at the horse museum at Château de Saumur and his memorial is at the Eaton Stud. Likewise honoured are **Lily Agnes** (1871–1899), **Orme** (1889–1915), **Shotover** (1879–99) and the St Leger winner **Touchstone** (1831–62), whose skeleton is at the stud. In his lifetime the first Earl Grosvenor is said to have accumulated more than £250,000 in gambling debts. Another family member bred **Copenhagen**, who carried the Duke of Wellington at Waterloo.

SANDIWAY

The **Blue Cap** pub sign commemorates a foxhound that died in 1772. In 1762 he won 500 guineas for his owner, John Smith–Barry, in a famous wager with Hugo Meynell, Master of the Quorn Hunt, and when Blue Cap died, a statue was erected at the Cheshire Kennels on the A556 bearing the words:

> If fame, honour and glory depend on the deed,
> Then O! Bluecap, we'll boast thy breed.

In 1999 plans for a new pub sign caused uproar when the dog depicted was said to look more like the cartoon character Snoopy.

WINCLE

An inscription on the Hanging Stone a short distance from St Lud's church marks the grave of **Burke**, a mastiff, pet of the Brocklehurst family of Swythamley Hall. He died in 1874. His epitaph reads:

> A noble mastiff, black and tan
> Faithful as woman, braver than man...

CORNWALL
BODMIN

After leaving Cambridge University, Prince Chula, cousin to the King of Siam, lived at Tredithy Manor, Helland. While there, he donated a dogs' drinking fountain in memory of **Joan**, a wire-haired terrier, and **Hercules**, a bulldog. The fountain is by the entrance to Priory Gardens, Bodmin. Prince Chula died in 1963.

MADRON

At Trengwainton, home of the Bolitho family, there was a tradition of burying hunters on the death of their owner. Having followed the funeral cortege to the gates, the master's horse was shot and buried beneath a magnolia tree.

Trengwainton Garden, Madron, near Penzance, Cornwall TR20 8RZ. National Trust. Telephone: 01736 363148.

MOUNT EDGCUMBE

On her death in 1909, Caroline Georgia, Countess of Mount Edgcumbe, requested that a fountain be erected on the shores of the river Tamar bearing the inscription 'for the doggies'. It stands close to the ferry point at Cremyll.

Cupid, the pet pig of Emma Gilbert, wife of George, first Earl of Mount Edgcumbe, is said to have travelled everywhere with his mistress. On his death about 1768, he was reputedly buried in a gold casket beneath a 30 foot obelisk erected on the former site of Mount Edgcumbe Folly. However, nothing was found when the monument was moved to its present position overlooking Plymouth Sound.

Graves dating from the late nineteenth century to the 1930s record other pets of the Edgcumbe family.

PENZANCE

The Penwith Horse Cemetery at Rose Farm, Chyanhal, near Penzance, is one of the few cemeteries to bury horses, each being placed beneath an apple tree. There is also an extensive small-animal cemetery, with public access.

ST AUSTELL

Heligan House (the name means 'willows' in Cornish) was built by William Tremayne in 1603. Extensive gardens were laid out in the nineteenth century but at the outbreak of the First World War the twenty-two male garden staff joined the

At the Penwith Horse Cemetery near Penzance apple trees mark horses' graves.

Duke of Cornwall's Light Infantry. Only six returned. The gardens subsequently fell into disuse but they were restored at the end of the twentieth century and, as 'The Lost Gardens of Heligan', are a popular visitor attraction. Columns to **Tony** (1873), **Lulu** (1890) and **Toto** (1894), three dogs of unknown breed belonging to the Tremaynes, remain.

The Lost Gardens of Heligan, Pentewan, St Austell, Cornwall PL26 6EN. Telephone: 01726 845100. Website: www.heligan.com

Memorial pillars to dogs at The Lost Gardens of Heligan near St Austell.

The pet cemetery at Dalemain in Cumbria.

CUMBRIA
BROCKHOLE
In the grounds of the Cragwood Hotel, near the Lake District National Park Visitor Centre between Windermere and Ambleside, stands a single headstone to **Pat, Tawney** and **Peter**, long-forgotten pets of a past owner.

BUTTERMERE
Two graves above Hassness House record the lives of dogs **Brandy** and **Patch**.

DALEMAIN
Graves of **Dalemain Nettle**, a Fell stallion, and various family dogs are in the grounds of Dalemain, home of the Hassell family since 1679.
Dalemain, Penrith, Cumbria CA11 0HB. Telephone: 017684 86450. Website: www.dalemain.com

DOW CRAG
In his book *The Southern Fells*, Alfred Wainwright mentions a simple dedication to **Charmer**, a foxhound killed in a fall at Dow Crag. The location was deliberately not disclosed.

THIRLMERE
By the roadside wall of the busy A591 is a memorial plaque to an unnamed coach horse that died in 1843.

WINDERMERE

Graves of horses in the grounds of Hird House, Patterdale Road, include: **Cobby**, 'killed at Ypres whilst serving his country April 1915', **Rajah** (4th February 1905), **Cossack** (February 1908), **Major** and **Minor**, 'for 20 years comrades and friends Dec 23 1909', and **Lord Roberts** (1899–1934), 'faithful friend'. Among the dogs are **Angus**, and two terrier friends, **Jock** and **Chippy**.
The house is now a Cheshire Home and the park is occupied by the Lakeland Horticultural Society.

DERBYSHIRE
BURBAGE

A 7 foot pillar, each face carved with the names of **Bob, Bold, Mona** and **Nell** stands at Burbage, near Buxton. Whom they belonged to is unclear – some say a farmer, others a silk merchant.

CROMFORD

A plaque on Cromford Bridge records the miraculous survival of a horse and Mr Benjamin Heywood, the rider, who jumped 20 feet into the Derwent in June 1697.

DERWENT RESERVOIR

In December 1953 Joseph Tagg, an 86-year-old shepherd, died on Howden Moor. His body was found fifteen weeks later, along with **Tip**, his sheepdog, who had remained with her master, enduring hunger and terrible weather. Tip was taken in by Mr Tagg's niece and died a year later. In recognition of Tip's devotion, a monument was erected by public donation near the spot by Derwent Reservoir.

MATLOCK

Commemorated by a plaque dated 1897 in St John's Chapel is **Vida**, the pet of Mrs Louise Sophie Harris. The chapel was supposedly built when Vida was refused a place in the village churchyard. Although unconsecrated, the chapel was used as a place of worship. The plaque on the chapel wall states: 'In most loving memory of Vida, till the last and brightest Easter Day be born.' Mrs Harris died in 1908, leaving £2000 to the RSPCA and Battersea Dogs' Home.

MONYASH

A stone outside Cross Lane Farm, Monyash, commemorates 'A loyal canine companion'.

TIDESWELL

A **cat** was carved by masons on a ledge of the tower of the Church of St John the Baptist. It is believed to represent one that climbed the scaffolding to inspect the stonework, but some say that as it is on the north side, and dates from a superstitious age, it may have symbolised evil.

DEVON
ARLINGTON

Arlington Court, in the hands of the Chichester family since 1384, was last occupied by Miss Rosalie Chichester (1865–1949), eccentric aunt of Sir Francis Chichester. **Polly**, her parrot, died in 1919 and was buried in the grounds. His

portrait is on display in the house. **Vanguard**, a dog who died in 1868, is remembered by a pedestal with panels on each side stating:
> The rich man's guardian and the poor man's friend,
> The only creature faithful to the end.

A statue of Miss Chichester's dog **Memory**, who died aged thirteen, tops Vanguard's pedestal.

Little Sandy and **Dick VI,** mother and son, died in 1889 and 1895 respectively. A block of red stone marks their grave with a verse from 'All Things Bright and Beautiful'.
Arlington Court, Arlington, near Barnstaple, Devon EX31 4LP. National Trust. Telephone: 01271 850296.

BIDEFORD

At Tapeley Park Gardens is a headstone to **George**, 'died November 16 1905, possessed of immortal virtues, conscience, love, constancy'.
Tapeley Park and Gardens, Instow, Bideford, Devon EX39 4NT. Telephone: 01271 342588. Website: www.tapeleypark.com

BRIXHAM

Along the coastal path between Berry Head and Man Sands is a wayside marker to **Murdoch**, 'my soul mate', in memory of the happy walks shared.

SIDMOUTH

The Donkey Sanctuary at Sidmouth, founded in 1969, has taken in 11,500 donkeys and provides help and training in donkey welfare worldwide. It is dependent upon gifts from the public, and memorials along the pathways provide valuable income. There is no charge for entry.
The Donkey Sanctuary, Sidmouth, Devon EX10 0NU. Telephone: 01395 578222. Website: www.thedonkeysanctuary.org.uk

A marker by a seat on the Devon coastal path near Brixham recalls the dog Murdoch.

SWIMBRIDGE

The pub sign at Swimbridge commemorates the Reverend Jack Russell, who established the familiar breed of dog. Born in Dartmouth in 1795, Russell acquired a terrier dog, whom he called **Trump**, from a milkman. From this beginning he perfected what he felt to be the ideal dog for flushing out foxes. The breed interested Edward VII sufficiently for him to commission a painting of Trump, which is now at Sandringham, where Russell sometimes preached. Russell was a founder member of the Kennel Club. He died at Swimbridge in 1883 and is buried in St James's churchyard.

DORSET
ABBOTSBURY

Laura, Tess, Stella and other yellow retrievers belonging to the family of the Earl of Ilchester, who developed the breed, are buried in what was originally the kitchen

Olympic gold medallist Cornishman V is buried near Cranborne in Dorset.

garden. Also buried is **Bruce**, a terrier belonging to Captain Loxley of HMS *Formidable*, torpedoed in the English Channel in 1915. Bruce was washed ashore and found on the beach.

Abbotsbury Sub-tropical Gardens, Bullers Way, Abbotsbury, Dorset DT3 4LA. Telephone: 01305 871387.

CRANBORNE

Cornishman V won two Olympic team gold medals, ridden by Richard Meade in Mexico City (1968) and by his owner, Mary Gordon Watson, at Munich (1972). He died aged twenty-seven and is buried beneath a slate panel at East Blagdon Farm near Cranborne.

Private residence.

DORCHESTER

Thomas Hardy doted on **Wessex,** a scruffy black and white puppy bought by his wife. **Wessex** slept with his master and at meal times jumped on to the table, challenging guests for their food. Only T. E. Lawrence, a frequent visitor, could handle him. Wessex died on 27th December 1926, aged thirteen, and was buried in the Hardys' garden at Max Gate. Then frail himself, Hardy mourned his pet until his own death in January 1928. Hardy was cremated and buried in Westminster Abbey, except for his heart, which is at Stinsford nearby. Wessex's headstone recalls a 'faithful unflinching' friend.

Max Gate, Alington Avenue, Dorchester, Dorset DT1 2AA. National Trust. Telephone: 01305 262538.

Thomas Hardy's dog is buried at Max Gate in Dorchester.

Animal graves in the grounds of Kingston Lacy.

KINGSTON LACY

Kingston Lacy, the seventeenth-century home of Sir Charles Barry, formerly of Corfe Castle, was in the nineteenth century the home of William Bankes. In the extensive grounds stand two gravestones, one to **Silvertail**, a pony that died in 1915, and one to 'Two old friends', who were buried together in 1896. Equine successes were recorded with mounted horseshoes on a door at the stables.

Kingston Lacy, Wimborne Minster, Dorset BH21 4EA. National Trust. Telephone: 01202 883402.

MELBURY SAMPFORD

There are over forty animal graves in the grounds of Melbury House, while in the chapel is the recumbent figure of Denzil Fox-Strangeways, who died at the

St Mary's church at Melbury Sampford is now the private chapel of Melbury House. The 1901 effigy of Denzil Fox-Strangeways has his bemused terrier as a foot rest.

beginning of the twentieth century; a terrier lies at his feet.
The grounds of Melbury House are occasionally open to the public.

WIMBORNE ST GILES

A **robin** is commemorated in the window to the south of the high altar in Wimborne St Giles church. The dedication states that: 'Here while the respond to the arcade of A. D. 1887 was building a robin nested and again during the building of the new arcade after the fire of 1908.'
It was decided to embed the second nest in the wall and this exposed the first nest in a bottle. Both are now in the wall.

COUNTY DURHAM
EGGLESTON

The site of Eggleston Hall near Barnard Castle has a long history and was once the home of the Earls of Westmorland. When the redundant church of the Holy Trinity was returned to the estate, there was a chance that it would fall into total neglect. Instead, visitors to the 4 acre Eggleston Hall Gardens can peer through the church windows at the dedications and wander around the restored churchyard. Among the renovated graves is a row of burials to some non-human residents, including a parrot, **Polly**, who died aged thirty years; **Bruce**, ' a faithful friend', who died in 1928; and **Mariner**, who departed this life in 1896 at the age of eighteen. Also

On the edge of the restored churchyard at Eggleston Hall Gardens are graves of family pets, including Polly.

present is 'Our dear dog **Manny**', who died in 1871. The lovely walled garden also contains the remains of four Jack Russells that belonged to the gardener.
Eggleston Hall Gardens, Barnard Castle, County Durham DL12 0AG. Telephone: 01833 650155. Website: www.egglestonhall.co.uk

RABY CASTLE

In the 1840s, as explorers returned from expeditions abroad with tiger skins for trophies, the Duchess of Cleveland commissioned her own, more modest rug. When her spaniel **Sally** died, the Duchess had her skin fashioned into a lap rug, which now lies in front of the fireplace.
Raby Castle, Staindrop, County Durham DL2 3AH. Telephone: 01833 660202. Website: www.rabycastle.com

SOUTH SHIELDS

John Simpson Kirkpatrick was born into a poor family in South Shields in 1892. In 1910 he emigrated to Australia, jumping ship and calling himself John Simpson. He worked first on a sugar plantation, then on a sheep station, and later became a fireman aboard the ship *Kooringa*. In 1914 he enlisted in the army and was sent to

John Kirkpatrick and his donkey are commemorated not only in South Shields, where he was born, but also on the Australian War Memorial in Canberra.

Gallipolli as a stretcher-bearer. As a boy he had developed an affinity with animals, driving a milk float and helping with the donkeys on the beach. Now, faced with the carnage, he acquired a **donkey**, known variously as Murphy, Duffy or Abdul, and in twenty-four days he ferried three hundred wounded soldiers to safety along Shrapnel Gulley (or Snipers' Alley). On 19th May 1915 he was shot through the heart and killed but the donkey continued his journey. Kirkpatrick was buried at Hell Spit, being denied a Victoria Cross only as a result of a clerical error. The donkey became the pet of the Indian 6th Mountain Battery, and went with them when they were evacuated.

In Australia the pair became heroes. Three commemorative postage stamps celebrated their achievements and they featured both on a frieze in Gallipoli, and on the war memorial at Ararat, Victoria. There is a bronze of John and his donkey at the Australian War Museum in Canberra. In 1988 Kirkpatrick was finally honoured in South Shields and a fibreglass statue by Robert Riley was erected in the High Street paid for by public subscription. It is inscribed: 'John Simpson Kirkpatrick, "the Man with the Donkey", 202 Pte J Simpson, Aust Army Medical Corps, Born South Shields 6 July 1892, Died Gallipoli 19 May 1915. A Hero of the Great War.'

WYNYARD PARK

At Wynyard Park are tombstones and monuments to Lady Londonderry's dogs, including **Tess**, who died in 1896.

ESSEX
AUDLEY END

Audley End, an eighteenth-century mansion, stands on the site of a Benedictine abbey. It was acquired by Thomas Howard, first Earl of Suffolk, and enlarged to entertain James I but what survives is only a third of the size it was then. The **dog burials** are a 'modest arrangement of three slabs set into the lawn'. The house is administered by English Heritage.

Audley End House and Gardens, Saffron Walden, Essex CB11 4JF. English Heritage. Telephone: 01799 522842.

Jacko, amateur sleuth, discovered the whereabouts of his murdered mistress's body and was subsequently recruited by the Essex Constabulary. His stuffed remains are at the Essex Police Museum in Chelmsford.

CHELMSFORD

Jacko, a small dog, belonged to Camille Holland, a victim of the Moat Farm murders. A fifty-six-year-old spinster, Camille married Samuel Dougal, not knowing that both his previous wives had died in quick succession. He had been imprisoned for fraud and spent time in an asylum. The couple bought a remote farm at Clavering and later Dougal announced that his wife had gone away. After four years he came to the attention of the police when he forged a cheque drawn on her estate. **Jacko** helped the police in their enquiries and the body of Camille was found at a spot frequented by the dog. She had been shot. Dougal was hanged at Chelmsford gaol in July 1903. Jacko attached himself to the local police force and after his death he was stuffed. Nearly a century later he was rediscovered and returned to the Essex Police Museum, where he is on display.

Essex Police Museum, Headquarters, Chelmsford, Essex CM2 6DA. Telephone: 01245 457150. Website: www.essex.police.uk/museum Visits by appointment only.

ILFORD

In 1917 Maria Dickin, in need of occupation, took up social work in London's East End. While she was distressed by human misery, the suffering of animals also made her determined to act. Being able to afford veterinary fees for her own pet, she resolved to bring the same service to the poor, the result being the People's Dispensary for Sick Animals. With the outbreak of the Second World War Maria produced a medal that became known as the 'Animal VC'. It has been awarded to eighteen dogs, three horses, one cat and thirty-one pigeons. Many recipients were buried at the **PDSA Cemetery** in Ilford. Among the recipients of the medal were:

Gander, a Newfoundland dog, for service with the Royal Rifles of Canada in Hong Kong in 1941. He died removing a live grenade that landed near wounded soldiers.

Endal, who also received one of only two Blue Peter Gold Badges awarded for saving a life. (The other went to the Blue Peter dog Bonnie, 1999.)

Beauty, a wire-haired terrier, also awarded the Pioneer Medal normally reserved for humans, for helping to rescue injured victims of war. Beauty was given the

The most famous occupant of the PDSA Cemetery in Ilford is ship's cat Simon of HMS Amethyst, awarded the Dickin Medal in 1949.

freedom of Holland Park 'and all the trees therein'.

- **Ex Flight Sergeant Lewis**: this goat, mascot of the RAF Association, was buried with full military honours.
- **Simon**, a black and white cat, was found in Hong Kong by the captain of the sloop *Amethyst* and adopted as the ship's mascot. In 1949 the *Amethyst* was ordered up the Yangtse River, which was viewed as an act of aggression by the Chinese, who fired on the ship. There were many injured, including Simon, who suffered numerous gashes to his back and legs. On board, resources were lacking and, in spite of his injuries, Simon caught many of the rats that attacked the dwindling supplies, thus saving the crew from possible starvation. He was awarded a PDSA medal for gallantry and received so much mail that a 'cat officer' had to be appointed to deal with it. The *Amethyst* returned to a hero's welcome but sadly Simon had to go into quarantine and, either from ill health or unhappiness, he died. He was buried with full naval honours, his coffin draped in a Union Jack. He was only three years old.

PDSA Cemetery, Woodford Bridge Road, Ilford, Essex.

GLOUCESTERSHIRE AND BRISTOL
BERKELEY

Countless people owe their lives to **Blossom**, a cow who fortuitously passed on cow pox to a young dairymaid, Sarah Nelmes. It was this that led Sir Edward Jenner to discover that the disease protected those who had had it against the far more deadly smallpox. Blossom's portrait is at the Jenner Museum

Jenner Museum, The Chantry, Berkeley, Gloucestershire GL13 9BN. Telephone: 01453 810631. Website: www.jennermuseum.com

BLOCKLEY

At Fish Cottage a tablet in the wall commemorates the pet **trout** of William Keyte. It reads:

Under the soil
The old fish do lie
20 years he lived and then did die
He was so tame
You understand
He would come and
Eat out of your hand.
Died April 20th 1855
Aged 20 years.

BRISTOL

In 1884 Mark Barraud, a scenery designer in Bristol, adopted a stray bull terrier cross puppy, naming him **Nipper** after his tendency to bite. When Mark died, Nipper went to Liverpool with Mark's brother Francis. Francis, a painter, noticed Nipper's fascination with his phonograph but it was not until three years after the dog's death that he transferred the image to canvas, naming it *Dog Looking at and Listening to a Phonograph*. The Royal Academy turned it down.

In 1899 the Gramophone Company suggested he replace the phonograph with a gramophone, offering him £100 for the painting plus the copyright. His Master's Voice was born. Francis, who died in 1924, painted twenty-four versions of the picture but the original hangs in the EMI headquarters at Gloucester Place, London. Nipper's image subsequently appeared on items from letter-openers to ladies' powder compacts. In 1990 HMV found a Nipper lookalike called Toby to promote their image but he was banned from entering Crufts. In 2000 a blue plaque commemorating Nipper's birthplace was unveiled on the wall of Bristol University at Park Row, on the corner with Woodlands Road. Nipper died in Kingston upon Thames, Surrey (*q.v.*).

One of the few cats interred in a churchyard, **Tom** was resident for fifteen years at St Mary Redcliffe, regularly accompanying the choir into church. When he died his funeral included organ music. The verger, the vicar and churchwardens escorted him to his place of rest. His gravestone states: 'The Church Cat 1912–27.' He is remembered in a sonnet by Gilbert Croker.

CHELTENHAM

Three Cheltenham Gold Cup Winners have statues at Cheltenham Racecourse.

Golden Miller (1927–57) won the Gold Cup five times and the Grand National once. Owned by Dorothy Paget, he is buried at Elsingham Stud, Bishop's Stortford.

At Bristol University a statue and blue plaque commemorate Nipper, the His Master's Voice dog.

His bronze statue on a brick pedestal is by Judy Boyt.

Arkle (1957–70), belonging to the Duchess of Westminster, was named after a mountain in Sutherland. His bronze statue by Doris Lindner (1971) overlooks the parade ring. His skeleton is at the National Racehorse Museum at the National Stud, Tully, County Kildare, Ireland.

A statue of **Dawn Run** and its jockey, Jonjo O'Neill, by Jonathan Knight, was unveiled at the racecourse paddock in 1987.

Cheltenham Racecourse, Prestbury Park, Cheltenham, Gloucestershire GL50 4SH. Telephone: 01242 513014. Website: www.cheltenham.co.uk.

In the town between Berkeley Street and Hewlett Road stands a fountain inscribed: 'Presented to the Corporation by the Ladies Society for Protection of Animals 1883 M Champion, Treasurer "The Lord is Good to All" Psalm CXLV v.9'.

FAIRFORD

Tiddles, a tabby cat at the Church of St Mary the Virgin, was befriended by the verger and his wife and stayed for seventeen years. She attended services, sitting on the knees of members of the congregation. When she died, Peter Juggins, a local stonemason, carved her likeness with the words 'Tiddles, the church cat, 1963–1980'. It is placed opposite the church porch.

HIGHNAM

Highnam Court, once the home of the composer Hubert Parry, has a pet cemetery by the pathway that leads to Holy Innocents church.

STROUD

In the woods surrounding Nether Lypiatt Manor, near Stroud, stands a small obelisk erected to **Wag**, who died in 1721. The inscription reads:

Outside the beautiful Perpendicular church at Fairford, noted for its stained glass windows, is a stone to Tiddles.

My name is Wag, who rolled the green,
The oldest horse that was ever seen,
My age it numbered forty-two,
I served my Master just and true.

The house, built in 1702, is a Grade I listed building.

TETBURY

By the entrance to the kitchen garden at Highgrove House is a carving of **Tigga**, Prince Charles's sixteen-year-old Jack Russell, who died in 2003. The dog, in Ham stone, is curled up and appears to be asleep. A nearby mound marks the grave.

Highgrove House is the home of HRH The Prince of Wales. Access is strictly limited.

HAMPSHIRE

ALDERSHOT

An **equine military cemetery** near the golf course at Shoe Lane contains five burials dating between 1880 and 1889. One was the charger of the Duke of Connaught, son of Queen Victoria. The cemetery, now neglected, is difficult to locate.

Copenhagen carried the Duke of Wellington to victory at Waterloo. Matthew Wyatt was commissioned to carve a statue of Copenhagen and the Duke to top the triumphal arch at Hyde Park. The statue, weighing 40 tons, took thirty men three years to complete. When it was unveiled, there were objections that the horse looked nothing like Copenhagen. The horse having died before the sculptor started work, he used a mare called Rosemary as a model.

Decimus Burton, who designed the triumphal arch, objected to the statue as being out of proportion but, in deference to Wellington, it was erected. When traffic congestion at Hyde Park became too great the arch was removed to Constitution Hill and the statue to Aldershot. A site was chosen on Round Hill, near the Royal Garrison Church, where it was erected in 1885.

ALRESFORD

Hambone Junior, a 'gingery mongrel with black patches', was the mascot of the 47th Infantry Regiment of the 9th Division, US Army, based at Alresford in 1944, but he was run over by a lorry. His grave was marked by two successive wooden crosses, replaced in 1962 by a memorial stone unveiled by the American vice consul at Southampton. The plaque to Hambone stands near the old eel houses, by Ladywell Lane on the banks of the river Alre. The dedication states: 'Here lies Hambone Jnr faithful friend of the 47th Infantry regt 9th Division U.S. Army May 1944'.

Sooty, a black Labrador-Alsatian cross, belonged to volunteers on the Mid-Hants Railway, alias the Watercress Line. He died one Christmas while they were staying on site and was buried close by. His headstone can be seen from the train.
Mid-Hants Railway (The Watercress Line), Alresford Station, Alresford SO24 9JG. Telephone: 01962 733810. Website: www.watercressline.co.uk

BRAMDEAN

There are conflicting stories about two

At Alresford in Hampshire are gravestones to Hambone Junior and Sooty, the railway dog.

Horse burials either side of the road at Bramdean: the mound in the foreground and the sarsen stones beyond.

horses buried along the A272 road near Bramdean. The first dates from the 1830s, when Colonel George Greenwood buried his favourite hunter, marking the spot with a burial mound. Colonel Greenwood wrote a book, *Hints on Horsemanship*, published in 1839.

On the opposite side of the road, a second memorial dates from the beginning of the twentieth century. Here a pile of sarsen stones is said to mark the burial place of **Melksham**, a favourite carriage horse belonging to Daniel (or Richard) Meinertzhagen of Brockwood Park, later tenant of Mottisfont Abbey. It is also claimed that these stones commemorate the burial of Colonel Greenwood's hunter.

EXBURY

The 200 acre garden of Exbury House, famous for rhododendrons and azaleas, was bought by the banker Lionel Rothschild in 1919 from the Mitford family. During the war it was used as HMS *Mastodon*, featuring in Nevil Shute's book *Requiem for a Wren*. In the grounds are gravestones to:

Scott, 'Who really smiled when pleased', a black Labrador, the pet of the owners, Edmund and Anne de Rothschild.

Joshua, 'Loved and missed by everyone', a golden Labrador belonging to Anne de Rothschild.

Fudge, 'As dear and sweet as his name'.

Ringo, 'A truly noble dog, loved by every age group'.

Jip, 'Our dear and faithful friend 1958–72'.

Nannie's Dear, Wee **Dougal**, 1962–75.

Exbury Gardens, Exbury, Southampton SO45 1AZ. Telephone: 023 8089 1203. Website: www.exbury.co.uk

FARLEY MOUNT

Beware Chalk Pit was the unusual name given to a horse belonging to Paulet St John. While they were out hunting, the horse leapt into a deep chalk pit but both

Dogs' gravestones at Exbury Gardens.

survived. St John erected a pyramid on a burial mound at Farley Mount Country Park with a memorial plaque stating 'Underneath lies buried a horse, the property of Paulet St John, that in the month of September 1733 leaped into a chalk pit twenty-five feet deep a foxhunting with his master on his back and in October 1734 he won the Hunters Plate on Worthy Downs and was rode by his owner and entered in the name of "Beware Chalk Pit".'

This event was also commemorated by Brooke Bond when launching their pyramid-shaped tea bags; they issued a tea card showing a chimpanzee riding a horse in front of the memorial.

This monument at Farley Mount, west of Winchester, commemorates the horse 'Beware Chalk Pit' buried beneath it.

SOUTHAMPTON

At the age of five, **Warrior**, a 16 hand grey gelding, was sent to France to serve with the Old Contemptibles. He suffered shrapnel wounds but remained there until the Armistice. Returned to Southampton, he was bought by Miss Hilda Moore and presented to the city, along with a bag of sugar, in recognition of his service. He became a familiar figure, pulling the Black Maria. Warrior died aged twenty-six and was buried in a general pit but later removed and given an individual grave surrounded by a garden at Southampton Golf Course.

His epitaph states: 'Warrior, died August 1935 aged 26 years. Served with the Old Contemptibles from 1914 until the end of the war. He took part in the retreat from Mons and was wounded in the advance on the Aisne. After the shrapnel was removed he returned for several further actions until the Armistice. He was purchased by Miss Hilda Moore and presented to the town. He at once assumed the chief position in the Police stud and was loved by all, not only for his famous war record but also for his intelligence, gentleness and noble character.'

STRATFIELD SAYE

Copenhagen, the horse ridden by the Duke of Wellington at Waterloo, was buried at Stratfield Saye and the music room is dedicated to his memory. Wellington was not sentimental about his horse but he did say that: 'There may have been many faster horses, no doubt many handsomer, but for bottom and endurance I never saw his fellow.'

Stratfield Saye House, Basingstoke, Hampshire RG7 2BZ. Telephone: 01256 882882. Website: www.stratfield-saye.co.uk

WINCHESTER

At the junction of Jewry Street with St George's Street there is a drinking trough dedicated 'In memory of the horses killed in the South African War 1899–1902. Given by Mrs Clowes.'

WOOLTON HILL

Gainsborough (1915–45) was the winner of the 1918 2,000 Guineas, the Derby and the St Leger. The sire of the great horse Hyperion, Gainsborough is buried at the Gainsborough Stud.

HEREFORDSHIRE
LUGWARDINE

In the 1880s a stone memorial to an unknown **horse** was discovered in the cellar of Longworth Hall. Now reinstated, it stands in the grounds, overlooking the river Frome. Longworth Hall is now a hotel.

MUCH BIRCH

In the late summer of 1981 **Muff**, a black, long-haired stray cat, arrived at The Laskett, home of Sir Roy Strong. He was named by Lady Strong, after

At Stratfield Saye, house of the Dukes of Wellington, is the grave of Copenhagen, who carried the first Duke 'the entire day' at the Battle of Waterloo.

The monument to the cat Muff at the home of Sir Roy Strong in Much Birch.

Wenceslas Hollar's painting of a lady's muff. In the autumn of 1992 he was bitten by a feral cat and died of feline AIDS. Muff was buried behind the Sugar Loaf yew in the garden, in a quiet spot close to a favourite walk called Sir Muff's Parade. Reg Boulton designed a reconstituted stone pedestal topped by a golden ball, the pedestal recalling Muff's attributes.
Private residence.

HERTFORDSHIRE
NORTH MYMMS

Horse-racing is a gamble, and the very existence of **Eclipse,** the racehorse, was down to chance. A chestnut colt bred by the Duke of Cumberland, he was born on 1st April 1764 during a solar eclipse. His dam, Spiletta, had never raced and failed to foal the year before, so the Duke had little hope of success. In addition, Eclipse's grandsire, called by the uninspiring name of Squirt, suffered so badly from laminitis, a painful and sometimes fatal foot condition, that his owner had ordered him to be shot. Only the intercession of the groom at the eleventh hour saved him. The Duke died a year after Eclipse was foaled and the bad-tempered colt was nearly gelded. At the age of five he had his first race. Trials were run in secret but an old lady, seeing the great animal thundering past, reported that no one would have caught him had he raced to the ends of the earth. When his potential became obvious, he came to the attention of Dennis O'Kelly, an Irish gambler who had once been a sedan chairman and had

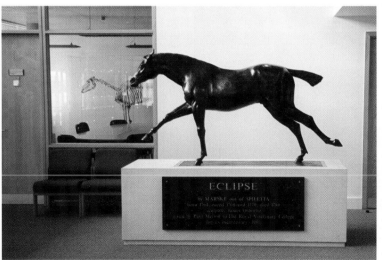

In the foyer of the Royal Veterinary College at North Mymms is a statue of Eclipse, the renowned thoroughbred. His skeleton is in the museum beyond the window.

been incarcerated in the Fleet Prison for debt. In a famous wager he offered to predict the outcome of Eclipse's next race, not only the winner but the rest of the field. This was achieved because the horse won by a distance, outclassing his competitors by at least 240 yards, thereby disqualifying the rest. Eclipse proved unbeatable, winning all of his eighteen races, and after two seasons retired to stud, making O'Kelly fabulously rich

The O'Kelly stud was at Clay Hill at Epsom but he also bought himself a stately home at Canons Park in Middlesex (now the North London Collegiate School). Here the elderly Eclipse was retired, travelling in a horse-drawn carriage – the first recorded horse-box! When Eclipse died in 1789, a wake was held in his honour. He sired the winners of 862 races, including three Derby winners, and 97 per cent of all thoroughbreds in training today descend through the male line to this amazing horse. His body was dissected to discover the secret of his speed and staying power and his skeleton is now in the museum of the Royal Veterinary College. A bronze statue of Eclipse, sculpted by James Osborne, was given to the college for the horse's bicentenary by Paul Mellon.

Royal Veterinary College, Hawkshead Lane, North Mymms, Hertfordshire AL9 7TA. Telephone: 01707 666333. Website: www.rvc.ac.uk

ST ALBANS

In appreciation of its horses, the **Childwick Bury Stud** erected monuments to its most successful residents, including: Crystal Palace (1956), Royal Palace (1964–91), winner of nine races; Humorist, winner of the 1921 Derby; Sunstar (1908–26), winner of the 1911 2000 Guineas; Sundridge (1898–1923), founder of the stud; and

Jim Joel's stud at Childwick Bury north of St Albans had many successes and this monument is to Doris (1898–1917), who foaled many winners.

Doris (1898–1917). Her monument records that: 'Among her many foals were the winners Little Dolly, Lady Portland, White Star, Bright, Selsey Bill, Radiant, Silver Star, Princess Dorrie (winner of the 1,000 Guineas) and Sundridge (2,000 Guineas)'.

TRING
Mick the Miller, the famous black greyhound, was born in Ireland in June 1926 and was named for the lad who cared for him as a puppy. The dog nearly died of distemper aged ten months. Mick won two English Derbys, later being bought for 2000 guineas. In total he competed in sixty-one British races, winning forty-six, coming second in ten, and had nineteen consecutive wins, gaining over £10,000 in prize money. He broke four world records in six weeks and had a starring role in a 1934 film, *Wild Boy*. Mick died on 5th May 1939. He was stuffed and is now on show at the Walter Rothschild Zoological Museum.
Walter Rothschild Zoological Museum, Akeman Street, Tring, Hertfordshire HP23 6AP. Telephone: 020 7942 6171. Website: www.nhm.ac.uk/visit-us/galleries/tring

ISLE OF WIGHT
BONCHURCH
In the grounds of the Lake Hotel, formerly known as Orchard Leigh, are tombstones to **Sporran**, killed by a car in 1929, and **Jess**, died 1930. This Georgian house once belonged to Dr Munro, who during the 1870s and 1880s rented it out for extensive periods to wealthy visitors, among whom was the Marchioness of Queensbury.

BRADING
The bullring preserved at Brading, and giving its name to the square, is a grisly reminder of the time when bull-baiting was a regular occurrence. It was in use until 1820. It was once illegal not to bait a bull before slaughter. Butchers failing to do so could be fined.

BROOK
Warrior was present at the battles of the Marne, Ypres, the Somme and Cambrai,

The bullring at Brading on the Isle of Wight.

surviving unscathed. Dubbed 'the horse the Germans couldn't kill' by the *Daily Telegraph*, he was also described as 'one of the greatest horses in history'. Warrior had been foaled in the spring of 1908 at Yafford on the Isle of Wight. A smallish, dark brown gelding with a white star, he was trained as a cavalry horse. He attended many victory parades and survived until 1941. When there was insufficient food available to give him the additional nourishment he needed, being now in his thirties, he was put down in the absence of his owner, Colonel Jack Seely, Lord Mottistone, who had been an MP and a government minister. In 1934 he had written a book about the animal, *My Horse Warrior*. When Warrior died, his obituary contained a quotation from Byron: 'I do not believe that he is denied in heaven the soul he held on earth.' His paddock is still known as 'Warrior's Field'.

CARISBROOKE

A stone set into the ground below the motte at Carisbrooke Castle commemorates **Wihtgar**, a St Bernard dog named after a Saxon buried at the castle in AD 544. The memorial tablet reads: 'In memory of Wihtgar, the beautiful S. Bernard of the late Captain Markland, former Custodian of Carisbrooke Castle, and the faithful companion of Mrs Markland till he died at Amherst on the 16th August 1899.' The castle is administered by English Heritage.

Donkeys have traditionally worked the wheel in the well-house at Carisbrooke Castle since the sixteenth century. Each donkey's name begins with a J and memorial stones placed on King Charles I's Bowling Green include: **Joe**, retired after twenty-five years of service, May 1960; **Jack**, died 1951 aged twenty-eight; **Jenny**, retired May 1862 aged nineteen; **Jack**, died 1st November 1923 aged twenty-six; and **Jacob**, died December 1959 aged ten.

Carisbrooke Castle, near Newport, Isle of Wight PO30 1XY. English Heritage. Telephone: 01983 522107.

Graves of the author's pets in her garden at Middleton, Freshwater.

FRESHWATER

Unusually, a house in the tiny hamlet of New Village is named after **Jeddah** (1895-1909), who won the 1898 Derby. He was owned and bred by James Lanarch and ridden by Otto Madden. Jeddah is buried at Lanwades Hall, Newmarket. His connection with the house in unclear. Jeddah Villa was formerly a blacksmith's forge.

Mardi, Herbie and Lucky, pets of the author, are buried in her garden at Middleton.

LAKE

At the top of the Fairway is a drinking trough dedicated 'To the horses and dogs who also bore the burden and heat of the day 1914–1920' (see page 10). On the other side are the words 'Be ye merciful'.

NEWPORT

Just outside Newport, in Pan Lane, the **Pets at Rest Cemetery** (see page 3) includes a chapel of rest. The ashes of several humans are interred with their pets. *Pets at Rest Cemetery, Pan Lane, Newport, Isle of Wight PO30 2PJ. Telephone: 01983 525335.*

NITON

When investigating the undergrowth surrounding their lovely old house at Niton, the Ward family discovered the graves of Chloe and Evadne, long forgotten pets of previous owners.

OSBORNE

Queen Victoria's youngest daughter, Princess Beatrice, was allowed to marry Prince Henry of Battenberg on the condition that the couple should live with the Queen. Much of their time was spent at Osborne House, the family retreat at East Cowes. Prince Henry, virile and restless, escaped to fight in South Africa, where he was killed in 1896. Beatrice remained with her mother until the Queen's death in 1901, serving as Governor of the island until her own death in 1944. **Bleny**, a pug dog, was buried under a cedar tree in the grounds of Osborne, where a stone commemorates the 'Favourite companion of Prince & Princess Henry of Battenberg died Dec 31 1893'.

Noble and **Sharp**, both collies, were carved in marble. Noble, sculpted by the Queen's talented daughter Princess Louise, is displayed in the corridor at Osborne House. When Noble died, the Queen, greatly distressed, declared that she believed dogs to have souls and, like humans, would meet in a future life. When the Queen died, her seventy remaining dogs were transferred by Edward VII to the kennels at Sandringham. *Osborne House, East Cowes, Isle of Wight PO32 6JY. English Heritage. Telephone: 01983 200022.*

At Barton Manor, the neighbouring home farm for Osborne House, lies another royal dog, **Morair**, a collie. His headstone states: 'Morair, son of Noble 2, grandson of Noble, Queen Victoria's favourite collie for 10 years, died March 1892 aged 7 years.'

Maggie and **Meme**, pets of a former owner of Barton Manor, were buried in the grounds in 1999 and 2001 respectively. Both dogs, mongrels, came from the RSPCA rescue centre. *Barton Manor is occasionally opened to the public for charity events.*

Gravestones at Barton Manor near Osborne House on the Isle of Wight.

KENT
FAVERSHAM

In the grounds of Belmont, a fine house built by the first Lord Harris in 1792, a line of pets' graves leads to the Prospect Tower, a Landmark Trust holiday let.
Belmont House and Gardens, Belmont Park, Throwley, Faversham, Kent ME13 0HH. Telephone: 01795 890202. Website: www.belmont-house.org.uk

LAMBERHURST

Maureen, Marchioness of Dufferin and Ava, acquired Owl House in 1952, designing the gardens herself. The tombstone of **Crocus Bud** (1947–61), a Pekinese, includes a poem written by the Marchioness:

Is there a country, Lord, where Thou dost keep
A place reserved for dogs that fall asleep?...
… I like to think there is, and so I pray
For one small dog of mine that died today,
He was so full of fun, not very wise,
The puppy look still lingered in his eyes.
But he was very dear, he'd come to me
And rest his soft black chin upon my knee.
Thou knowest him. One night not long ago
He tramped with me across the frozen snow
And there, beyond the wood peaceful and still
We met Thee walking on the moonlit hill.
Lord keep him safe wherever he may be,
And let him always have a thought of me…

Prospect Tower, once used as a cricket pavilion, overlooks the pets' graves at Belmont, near Faversham.

Below: *Crocus Bud's grave at Owl House, Lamberhurst.*

Kling Kling's grave commemorates 'The heavenly Peke, always here', while **Buddha's** grave states 'Coming back'. Also buried is **Topsy**, a poodle belonging to the Marchioness's daughter, Lady Perdita Blackwood, who died before her mother. The Marchioness, a member of the Guinness family, died aged ninety-one in 1998, requesting that the gardens remain open to the public.
Owl House Gardens, Lamberhurst, Kent TN3 8LY. Telephone: 01892 891290. Website: www.owlhouse.com

PETTS WOOD

A memorial plaque to **Yerba**, a police dog shot in a bank robbery at Lloyds Bank, Petts Wood, is in the Station Square. Yerba was killed on 15th August 1984 when a delivery vehicle was held up by two robbers. Yerba, sent to do a gun attack as trained, was shot and thrown back but attacked again and was shot a second time. He got to his feet a third time but collapsed and died. The robber shot him once more before making his escape. Yerba was buried at the Dog Training Establishment at Keston, Kent, and received an RSPCA Citation: 'For such courage the RSPCA Council unanimously decided that the Society's Plaque for Intelligence and Courage be awarded posthumously to Yerba. But for the actions of this brave animal, death or serious injury could have been sustained by other persons'. Yerba's handler ended his career as an explosive search dog handler at Nine Elms police station.

SMALLHYTHE

Inscriptions on the wall at Smallhythe Place commemorate **Ben** (1902–13), 'Dear dog', and **Toby** (1912–34), pets of the actress Ellen Terry.
Smallhythe Place, Smallhythe, Tenterden, Kent TN30 7NG. National Trust. Telephone: 01580 762334.

LANCASHIRE

AINTREE

Foaled on 3rd May 1965, **Red Rum** was found to be suffering from a crippling foot disease and was then sold by his owner, Mrs Brotherton, whose ambition was to win the Grand National, and bought on behalf of Noel Le Mare, who had the same aspiration. Red Rum's foot problem was cured by training in salt water on the beach at Southport. He ran in five Grand Nationals, winning the race in 1973, 1974 and 1977. He also won the 1974 Scottish Grand National. In 1978 he was withdrawn on the eve of his sixth Grand National when it was discovered that he had a hairline fracture.

Winner of the 1977 Sports Personality of the Year award, Red Rum toured Britain as a celebrity. He died on 18th October 1995 and was buried at the finishing line at Aintree racecourse. An engraved stone lists his Grand National achievements and there is a life-size bronze statue on the course. His sire, **Quorum**, is buried at the Littleton Stud, Hampshire.

BOLTON

Two identical tablets at Smithills Hall record the life of **Little Bess**, the dog of Colonel R. H. Ainsworth. Each states: 'Multum in parvo. In memory of Little Bess, in whom we lose sagacity, love and fidelity. She was of the rarest beauty and though smallest of her race, yet was possessed of the most lion hearted courage. Obiit Jan. 13, 1873. Aetat 6.'
Smithills Hall, Dean Road, Bolton BL7 7NP, is administered by the Smithills House and Garden Trust. Telephone: 01204 332377.

BURY

Minnie the Mule was born in Burma in 1944, behind Japanese lines, where the 1st Battalion 20th Lancashire Fusiliers was serving. She arrived during a raid and this unexpected new life in the midst of death seemed symbolic. When the Fusiliers were posted to India, Minnie was flown there. Her antics endeared her to the soldiers and when they eventually returned to England she was transported home by ship. At the height of her career she attended numerous parades, including Trooping the Colour in 1948. On 8th November 1951 she developed pneumonia while serving in Ismailia and died. Her tail and hooves were retained, two of which

are on display at the regimental museum at Bury.
The Fusiliers Museum Lancashire, Wellington Barracks, Bolton Road, Bury, Lancashire BL8 2PL. Telephone: 0161 764 2208. Website: www.fusiliersmuseum-lancashire.org.uk

LIVERPOOL
In 1935, up to five thousand horses regularly delivered food and raw materials around Liverpool. During the war their work proved invaluable in keeping the city served with essential supplies. In recognition of their contribution a **Liverpool Carters' Working Horse Monument** is planned, to be designed by the equine sculptor Judy Boyt. While fund-raising continues, models of the proposed statue are on display at the Museum of Liverpool Life and at the Liverpool Municipal Buildings.
Museum of Liverpool Life, Pier Head, Liverpool L3 1PZ. Telephone: 0151 478 4080. Website: www.liverpoolmuseums.org.uk/liverpoollife

LEICESTERSHIRE
GADDESBY
St Luke's parish church, Gaddesby, contains a statue to Colonel Edward Hawkins Cheney (1778–1848), the only full-sized equestrian statue in an English church. Hawkins rode five horses at the Battle of Waterloo; four were killed and one wounded. The statue depicts **Tannar**, with a bullet wound in his chest. The base of the statue states: 'Tannar, one of four horses killed under him June 18 1815'. Tannar's teeth are blackened from having an apple inserted in its mouth at each Harvest Festival. Rumour states that the sculptor, Joseph Gott, failed to give the horse a tongue and as a result he committed suicide. Gott died in Italy – but seemingly from natural causes.

LUBENHAM
Mr J. B. Cherry Angel, a racehorse trainer of Lubenham, is reputed to have added a room to his house every time he had a winner – ending up with twenty-five bedrooms. In 1865 his horse **Alcibiade** won the Grand National. He had a tower constructed to commemorate the event. It was later saved from demolition by the Reverend Graham Dilley, the 'hunting parson'. Alcibiade was ridden by Mr Burton of Daventry, who was buried in Lubenham churchyard, the horse's grave being just over the wall. **Brown Jack** (1924–49), a popular racehorse, was also trained at Lubenham, winning twenty-five races in five years. When he died, his skeleton went to the Natural History Museum at South Kensington.

Tannar, depicted full-size with a bullet hole in his chest, at St Luke's church, Gaddesby.

MARKET BOSWORTH

Smut, a black and tan Old English terrier, belonged to Lady Florence Dixie. When he was killed in 1876, his grieving mistress erected a memorial in Portland stone with doves in the Wilderness at Bosworth Hall, which was then the family home. The memorial states: '…Here lies a friend never forgotten.' On the top of the plinth is a lengthy poem to:

> …The dearest truest friend I ever knew
> Forget me not I seem to hear thee say
> Forget thee never! Never while memory lives
> Can this sad heart do aught but dream of thee
> And tend with gentle love thy last repose…

Florence Dixie, youngest daughter of the seventh Marquis of Queensberry, was a poet, travel writer and campaigner for women's equality. A voracious hunter in her youth, she became opposed to blood sports and vivisection. Because of gambling debts, Bosworth Hall was sold and Florence is buried at the family's other seat, Kinmount in Dumfries. Also in the grounds is a memorial slab to **Teddy** – 'A much loved Lakeland Terrier'.

A column and a cairn mark horse burials in a field adjoining Market Bosworth Country Park. **Trumps** was the charger of Captain Norton Legge ARC, while the memorial to **Scots Grey**, a hunter, records '10 seasons without a fall'.

Below left: Bosworth Hall Hotel, Market Bosworth, was once the home of Lady Florence Dixie, who in 1876 erected this impressive memorial to her dog Smut.

Below right: Market Bosworth Country Park occupies the site of a seventeenth-century deer park, and two monuments to horses are in an adjoining field.

MELTON MOWBRAY

At the Defence Animal Centre is a commemorative slab (see page 10) to **Sefton**, hero of the 1982 Hyde Park bombings. Suffering sixteen shrapnel wounds, he was treated at the centre and returned to service. Later he retired to the Home of Rest for Horses at Speen, Buckinghamshire, where he died in July 1993, aged thirty.

LINCOLNSHIRE
BROCKLESBY

A memorial urn erected at Brocklesby to **Dashaway**, who belonged to Charles Worsley Pelham, fourth Earl of Yarborough (1859–1936), bears the inscription: 'Under this urn lies Dashaway, a favourite hunter aged 21 years, 1891.' The Earl insisted on a nightly ritual whereby the butler reported: 'The horses are bedded down, m'lord.' Any dinner guests were then taken to inspect the stables.

LINCOLN

Simon, belonging to Colonel Ellison of Boulton Hall, was taken to the Crimea and was one of the few horses to return. The colonel erected a vista monument in his honour and when the hall was demolished in 1959 it was removed to Simon's Green, on the Simon's Hill Estate. Suggestions that Simon was buried beneath the monument proved to be untrue.

SCAMPTON

A black Labrador called 'Nigger', belonging to Guy Gibson VC, was the squadron mascot at RAF Scampton and often accompanied his owner on training flights. On the evening of 16th May 1943, as raids on the Eider and Mohne Dams were carried out, the dog was killed when he ran under a car. The incident was depicted in the film *The Dambusters*. He was buried at midnight as Gibson flew over the Mohne Dam, his grave being within sight of his owner's office. Guy Gibson was killed the following year in Holland.

Museum, RAF Scampton, near Lincoln. Telephone: 01522 879137. Visitors must book in advance.

Left: *South of Lincoln city centre, in a suburban cul-de-sac, is this monument to Crimean veteran Simon.*

Below: *The grave of Guy Gibson's dog at RAF Scampton.*

LONDON and MIDDLESEX
BATTERSEA

In 1902 the National Antivivisection Society erected a bronze statue above a fountain at the Latchmere Estate, dedicated to an unnamed terrier, referred to as **Brown Dog**, who suffered prolonged experimentation at University College. The statue became a focus for opponents of vivisection and more than £5000 was collected in support of Brown Dog. When the succeeding council decided to take his statue down there followed protests bigger than any until the Poll Tax demonstrations of the 1980s. An armed guard was placed on the statue but under cover of darkness it was thrown into the Thames. Brown Dog was not, however, forgotten and in 1985 a new statue by Nicola Hicks was erected, bearing the original inscription. It now stands in a quiet spot in Battersea Park, SW11, near to the Peace Pagoda (see page 7).

CHELSEA

Thomas Carlyle, known as the 'Sage of Chelsea', lived at 24 Cheyne Walk, SW3, from 1834 to 1881. The house, purchased by subscription in 1895, was opened to the public in 1896 and then transferred to the National Trust. Both Thomas Carlyle and his wife Jane worked in the walled garden and **Nero**, Jane's dog, was buried near the south-east corner in February 1860. The headstone is no longer extant.
Carlyle's House, 24 Cheyne Row, Chelsea, London SW3 5HL. National Trust. Telephone: 020 7352 7087.

CHISWICK

William Hogarth's talent for satire won him both praise and condemnation. His pug dog **Trump** often featured in his work, appearing in a self-portrait of the artist (1748). In 1763 Hogarth's attack on John Wilkes resulted in Hogarth in turn being lampooned, his face replaced by that of Trump. In response to a criticism in verse, *Churchill's Epistle to William Hogarth*, Hogarth portrayed Trump pissing on Churchill's verse. In his painting *Four Stages of Cruelty* he sought to shock people into being kinder to animals. The Huguenot sculptor Louis François Roubiliac made a model of Trump that was used as a figurine by the Chelsea porcelain factory. In 1999 a statue of Hogarth and Trump was placed near to Hogarth's house at the junction of Chiswick High Road and Annandale Road, W4. Ian Hislop and David Hockney unveiled the figure of the man while Trump was unveiled by a pupil from Hogarth Primary School.
Hogarth's House, Hogarth Lane, Chiswick, London W4 2QN. Telephone: 020 8994 6757.

CITY OF LONDON

A statue of **Dick Whittington**, four times Lord Mayor of London between 1397 and 1419, and his famous cat stands in a recess in the wall of the Guildhall Art Gallery.
Guildhall Art Gallery, Guildhall Yard, London EC2P 2EJ. Telephone: 020 7606 3030.

In 1936, Father Ross of the church of St Faith and St Augustine, Watling Street, EC4, took in a stray tabby kitten, naming her **Faith**. In August 1940 she gave birth to a single black and white tom kitten called Panda. On 6th September of that year Faith indicated that a basement door should be opened and she took the kitten down below. As it was cold and dark there, they were brought out but Faith

Laurence Tindall's sculpture of Dick Whittington and his cat at the Guildhall Art Gallery, London.

returned and hid Panda there. After a third attempt, her basket was taken into the basement and there she settled. There followed an air raid in which more than four hundred people died and two days later a severe raid hit eight churches, including St Faith and St Augustine's, which, with the exception of the tower, was razed. Faith and Panda were rescued moments before the roof collapsed. In memory of this event, Father Ross had Faith's photograph displayed on the chapel wall of the tower. The dedication praised: 'Faith: our dear little church cat … the bravest cat in the world…'. Faith was recommended for a PDSA medal but being a civilian cat she did not qualify. On hearing her story, however, Maria Dickin had a special silver medal made in her honour. The medal is inscribed: 'From the P.D.S.A to Faith of St Augustine's, Watling Street, E.C. For steadfast courage in the Battle of London, September 9th 1940.' The ceremony was carried out at the church on 12th October 1945, attended by Geoffrey Fisher, Archbishop of Canterbury. Faith lived to be about fourteen, dying quietly in her accustomed place on a rug by the fire. A service was held in the church and Faith was buried near the churchyard gate. St Augustine's tower is now part of St Paul's Cathedral Choir School.

In 1997 a statue of **Hodge,** Samuel Johnson's cat, was placed outside 17 Gough Square, EC4, where Johnson lived for eleven years while writing much of his dictionary. Space being limited, it was agreed that Hodge rather than his master should represent them. James Boswell, being scared of cats, admitted that he 'Suffered a good deal from the presence of this same Hodge'. Johnson concurred that Hodge was not his favourite but, seeing the cat's hurt expression, he added 'But he's a very fine cat, a very fine cat indeed'. These words appear on the plinth, where Hodge sits with oysters

Samuel Johnson's cat Hodge sits outside the Doctor's house off Fleet Street, London.

in front of him, on a copy of the famous dictionary. Johnson's own statue is outside St Clement Danes, the church he often attended.
Dr Johnson's House, 17 Gough Square, London EC4A 3DE. Telephone: 020 7353 3745. Website: www.drjh.dircon.co.uk

HAMPSTEAD GARDEN SUBURB

On the north side of the west door, in the church of St Jude on the Hill, Hampstead Garden Suburb, is a **Memorial to horses killed in the First World War**, consisting of a round plaque of a rearing horse. The present memorial was made in 1970 by Rosemary Proctor to replace one that was stolen and which in turn replaced an original bronze of a horse by Edwin Lutyens's father, also stolen.

HYDE PARK

Between 1880 and 1915 some three hundred pets were sewn into canvas bags and interred in the garden of the gatekeeper, Mr Windbridge. This evolved into **Hyde Park Cemetery.** The first burial was probably **Prince**, run over at the gate of the lodge and belonging to the Duchess of Cambridge. Alternatively, **Cherry**, a Maltese terrier and pet of the Lewis Barnard family, may have been the first, buried in the garden at the request of the children. Among the burials is **Topper**, a fox terrier and Metropolitan police dog who worked in the park (1893). Also buried are 'foreign' pets such as **Kulach**, born in Berne; **Pixie**, *'le Petit'*; **Bibi**, *'A doce Memorie do nosso querido catinho, 1901'*; **Prinnie**, a dachshund belonging to Colonel Montefiore; and **Kaiser**, a Spitz, bred in Germany and run over 5th April 1886. The cemetery is closed but a visit can be requested in advance from the Park Ranger (telephone: 020 7298 2100).

Some of the many graves at the Hyde Park pet cemetery.

KILBURN

Following the First World War, the **Peace Pledge Union** donated a house to the RSPCA at Cambridge Avenue, Kilburn, NW6, in memory of animals that died during the conflict. The house, used as a veterinary clinic, has a relief above the door and two plaques, one at each side. The first states:

> This building is dedicated as a memorial to the countless thousands of God's humble creatures who suffered and perished in the Great War 1914–18, knowing nothing of the cause, looking forward to no final victory. Filled only with love, faith and loyalty, they endured much and died for us. May we all remember them with gratitude and in the future commemorate their suffering and death by showing kindness and consideration to living animals.

The second plaque reads:

> This tablet records the deaths in enemy action, disease or accident of 484,222 horses, mules and bullocks and many hundreds of dogs, carrier pigeons and other creatures on the Front during the Great War. In France alone 725,216 sick and wounded animals were treated in the veterinary hospitals provided by the RSPCA.

LAMBETH

When the German ship *Dresden* was sunk off the Falklands in 1915, a large pig swam towards HMS *Glasgow*, waiting to be rescued. Originally called Dennis, he was renamed **Turpitz** and spent a year at sea, being adopted as the ship's mascot. On reaching England, he was sent to Whale Island in Portsmouth Harbour but he ate such huge quantities of food intended for the chickens that he was transferred to Cranwell. It took ten men to load him into a transporter. At Chester he was auctioned in aid of the Red Cross, the Duke of Portland paying £440 for him. Two months later he was auctioned again, this time in Ayrshire, raising £840 for the Agricultural Relief Fund. The Duke of Portland again bought him back and re-auctioned him at the Patriotic Fair at Nottingham. Here, Turpitz raised £505. When Turpitz died in 1919, his head was mounted and his trotters turned into carving sets, both being donated to the Imperial War Museum, SE1 (see page 9).

Jack was the pet of Edith Cavell (1865–1915), an English nurse who served in Belgium during the First World War. She helped two hundred Allied soldiers trapped behind enemy lines to escape, knowing that they would be shot if captured. Edith was tried by the Germans and executed by firing squad, wearing her nurse's uniform, on 12th October 1915. Her last words were 'I know now that patriotism is not enough. I must have no hatred, no bitterness towards anyone.' Jack was rescued by Princess Mary de Croy and taken to the Croy estate in Belgium. When he died in 1923 he was embalmed and

Edith Cavell's dog Jack has ended up at the Imperial War Museum, London.

returned to England, to the Norfolk branch of the Red Cross. He is now in the Imperial War Museum.
Imperial War Museum, Lambeth Road, London SE1 6HZ. Telephone: 020 7416 5320. Website: www.iwm.org.uk

PADDINGTON

In the year 2000 a model of **Paddington Bear** was unveiled at Paddington station by Michael Bond, the bear's creator. According to the stories, Paddington was found at the station, having arrived from darkest Peru. It stands beside the escalator to the underground.

PENGE

To the north-east of the railway bridge at Penge, SE20, and on the south-east side of Green Lane stands a drinking trough bearing the inscription: 'Be kind and merciful to all animals. In memory of David Benjamin 1815–1893.'

PINNER

A small dog cemetery dating from the nineteenth century is at the north-west entrance to Pinner Memorial Park, opened in 1950. West End Lodge, part of the grounds, was once occupied by Nelson's daughter, Horatia.

REGENT'S PARK

Perhaps the most famous past resident of London Zoo, **Guy the Gorilla** lived there from 1947 to 1978, having come from French Cameroon via France. A bronze statue by William Timyn was presented to the zoo after his death. It stands on the south side of the Michael Sobell Pavilion.

Guy the Gorilla was a major attraction at London Zoo in Regent's Park for more than thirty years.

Winnipeg, an American black bear, was resident at London Zoo from 1914 to 1934. The mascot of Canadian troops stationed in England, Winnipeg was donated to the zoo when they were posted to France. He was named after the city where he was found. A bronze sculpture shows the cub Winnie on a brick plinth, holding the hands of Captain Colebourn, who rescued him. The statue, at the south-west corner of the Reptile House, is by Lorna McKean. Winnipeg was the inspiration for A. A. Milne's Winnie the Pooh and the statue was unveiled by his son Christopher Milne, the 'Christopher Robin' of the books.

London Zoo, Regent's Park, London NW1 4RY. Telephone: 020 7722 3333. Website: www.londonzoo.co.uk

RUISLIP

On the site of an old motte and bailey at the **Manor Farm Complex** are plaques recording animal burials. There is unlimited access to the grounds, entered from the Bury Street/St Martin's approach.

Manor Farm Complex, Bury Street, Ruislip, Middlesex HA4. Telephone: 01895 250050.

SHEPHERD'S BUSH

A bust of **Petra** (1962–77), *Blue Peter's* original and most famous dog, stands in the Blue Peter Garden at the BBC Television Centre, Wood Lane, W12. It was created by William Timyn, who also sculpted Guy the Gorilla for London Zoo. **George** the tortoise was buried in the garden in May 2004. Other pets are interred in a Sussex garden, where they were looked after, while **Goldie** is buried at Simon Groom's parents' house in Derbyshire. **Bonnie** was cremated and her ashes were scattered in the Blue Peter Garden.

SOUTHWARK

On a traffic island in Queen Elizabeth Street, SE1, near Tower Bridge, stands a bronze statue of **Jacob**, sculpted by Shirley Pace at the Burleighfield Arts Foundry in about 1987. The plaque on the pedestal states: 'The famous Courage dray horses were stabled on this site from the early nineteenth century and delivered beer around London from the brewery on Horsely Down Lane by Tower Bridge. In the sixteenth century the area became known as Horsely-down, which derives from Horse-lie-down, a description of working horses resting before crossing London Bridge into the City of London. Jacob was commissioned by Jacobs Island Company and Farlane Properties as the centrepiece of the circle to commemorate

Jacob, the dray horse, by Shirley Pace, commemorates the horses at the Courage brewery in Southwark near Tower Bridge.

the history of the site. He was flown over London by helicopter into Queen Elizabeth Street to launch the circle in October 1987...' The architects were Campbell Zogolovitch Wilkinson and Gough, Robinson Keefe & Devane. The monument was completed in 1990.

ST JOHN'S WOOD

The King's Troop, Royal Horse Artillery, originally known as the Riding Troop, houses memorial stones to four horses. The oldest dates to 1808 and recalls **Wonder**, who died aged forty years, the mount of Captain Quist, riding master of the Riding House Department, appointed by King George III. The others commemorate: twenty-year-old **Leicester**, a mare who represented England in the Nice and Dublin international horse shows, died 1932; **Winstow**, died 1934 aged twenty-two, who also attended the same horse shows; and **Kayenne**, charger of G. W. Heath, 'a very gallant gentleman', who died aged seventeen in 1932. Some of the stones were moved from Aldershot and Woolwich.

TWICKENHAM

Strawberry Hill was the home of Horace Walpole, youngest son of Sir Robert Walpole, England's first and longest serving Prime Minister. When **Selima**, his cat, died, the poet Thomas Gray immortalised her in an *Ode on the Death of a Favourite Cat Drowned in a Tub of Goldfishes,* first published in 1748.

Madame Deffand, mistress of Philippe II, Duc d'Orleans, left her dog **Tonton** to Walpole, and Walpole left Strawberry Hill to the Honourable Anne Seymour Damer, an eccentric sculptor who specialised in models of miniature dogs.

WAPPING

At the old Tobacco Dock, Pennington Street, Wapping, E1, two fibreglass figures symbolise the days when ships arrived along the Thames from far and wide. A **tiger** commemorates an escape from Jamrach's Wild Animal Emporium, which stood on the site. The tiger was approached by a small boy who was stunned by a swipe from its paw. According to the story, the tiger carried the unconscious boy away and Mr Jamrach forced his hand into the animal's throat, making him let go. The tiger was then led quietly back to his cage.

Seafarers brought creatures to sell and these were housed by Jamrach for onward transmission to zoos or collectors. A statue of a large **bear**

The story of the boy and the tiger is illustrated at the Tobacco Dock in Wapping.

This memorial is to the Imperial Camel Corps of the First World War. A thousand camels were used and the Armistice cross tied to the camel's leg by a passer-by has a reminder to remember the poor animals.

stands opposite the tiger, a collecting point for donations to the World Wildlife Fund. The Tobacco Dock is a Grade 1 listed building.

WESTMINSTER

In the gardens east of Embankment Underground station, WC2, is a memorial plaque to the **Camel Corps**, incorporating a camel ridden by Major Cecil Brown. Camels saw service in the First and Second World Wars.

Princess Alexandra, wife of the future Edward VII, was passionate about animals and at Marlborough House, their London home, **Muff, Tiffany, Joss** and **Benny** (a rabbit) are all buried in the garden. Later, the king's extramarital affairs and Alexandra's increasing deafness left her isolated and when her dog **Togo**, a gift from the Empress of Japan, died, she was bereft. His tomb bears the words: 'My darling little Togo … my constant companion for twelve years. The joy and pleasure of my life, died May 25th 1914.'

The £1 million **Memorial to Animals Killed in War** has been funded by public subscription. Unveiled on 24th November 2004 at Brook Gate, Park Lane, W1, it was designed by David Backhouse and features two mules, a stallion and a dog before a curved Portland stone wall (see page 1). Even the service of glow-worms providing light in the trenches is acknowledged. An accompanying note on a wreath left at the opening ceremony stated: 'Forgive us, dear animals, that we have asked you to serve in this way in war.'

During the 1930s the German Embassy occupied numbers 7, 8 and 9 Carlton House Terrace, SW1. When **Giro**, the pet dog of the ambassador, Leopold von Hoesch, died in February 1934, he was buried behind railings at the top of the Duke of York Steps. A stone declares him to be *'ein trueur Begleiter'* ('a true companion').

Giro, the dog of the German ambassador, died in 1934 and is buried by the top of the Duke of York Steps.

Ambassador Hoesch suffered a stroke while in office in 1935 and before setting out for Germany from Victoria station he received a nineteen-gun salute in St James's Park. He died and was replaced by von Ribbentrop.

In June 1812 **Sancho**, a large white poodle, was found lying on the body of his French master and rescued from the battlefield at Salamanca by the Marquis of Worcester. Both the Marquis and the dog appear in a print, entitled 'Hyde Park', now hanging in the National Portrait Gallery.
National Portrait Gallery, St Martin's Place, London WC2H 0HE. Telephone: 020 7306 0055. Website: www.npg.org.uk

WIMBLEDON
The graves of 'a vast wolfhound', a black cat called **Loki** and an owl named **Romulo** are in the gardens at Southside House, Woodhayes Road, Wimbledon Common, SW19. The garden was created by Hilda Pennington-Mellor and Dr Axel Munthe, who occupied the house at the beginning of the twentieth century. It is now administered by the Pennington-Mellor-Munthe Trust and is open to the public.
Southside House, 3–4 Woodhayes Road, Wimbledon Common, London SW19 4RJ. Telephone: 020 8946 7643. Website: www.southsidehouse.com

NORFOLK
SANDRINGHAM
Set into a wall in the grounds of Sandringham are memorials to **dogs belonging to the Queen and the Duke of Edinburgh**. These include Candy, the 'Faithful companion of the HRH Duke of Edinburgh, died Sandringham Jan 12 1958', and Sandringham Brae, 'A gentleman among dogs', a black Labrador who died on 10th May 1992. Other memorials include Sandringham Salt and Sandringham Fern. Pets belonging to Queen Alexandra and King Edward VII lie at the end of the Rose Garden. Queen Alexandra, an admirer of the work of jeweller Karl Fabergé, commissioned him to make several models of her favourite dogs.

One is reminded of King Edward VII's passion for horse-racing by the statue of **Persimmon**, which won the 1896 Derby by a neck. Sent to Epsom by train, he refused to enter the van and had to be manhandled aboard. Twice champion sire, Persimmon's progeny were successful on both sides of the Atlantic. He died aged fifteen after suffering a broken pelvis. His head was mounted and is on display at the Newmarket horse-racing museum.
Shirley Heights (1975–97), winner of the 1978 Derby, is buried at the Royal Stud, Sandringham.
Sandringham House, Norfolk PE35 6EN. Telephone: 01553 612908. Website: www.sandringham-estate.co.uk

SNETTERTON
To aid fund-raising, the **International League for the Protection of Horses** has established a Trees in Tribute memorial park at Hall Farm, Snetterton. Over six hundred trees have been planted, providing welcome shelter for convalescing horses.
ILPH, Hall Farm, Snetterton, Norfolk NR16 2LP. Telephone: 0870 870 1927 (weekdays) or 01953 498898 (weekends). Website: www.ilph.org

NORTHAMPTONSHIRE
KETTERING

Charles Wicksteed, an engineer who made park benches and playground equipment, moved to Kettering from the north of England and founded Wicksteed Park in 1913 for the benefit of the local people. His dog, **Jerry**, a poodle, was his constant companion but on the one occasion his owner left him behind Jerry was stolen and Wicksteed never saw him again. One day, while he was on holiday, Wicksteed saw a statue in a shop that reminded him so much of Jerry that he had it shipped home and erected in the park. The memorial states:

To the memory of
JERRY
The constant companion of
Charles Wicksteed
1920–1928

Closely bound to human heart,
Little Brown Dog, you had your part
In the levelling, building, staying of streams
In the park that arose from your master's dreams.

Wicksteed died in 1931.

Wicksteed Park, Kettering, Northamptonshire NN15 6NJ. Telephone: 08700 621193. Website: www.wicksteedpark.co.uk

TOWCESTER

At Easton Neston, an elegant house designed by Nicholas Hawksmoor for Sir William Fermor, is an unusual memorial in the form of a stone slab mounted on two ornate legs. The slab bears the simple yet elegantly carved inscription 'To the memory of Pug'. The house is privately owned and is said to have been the inspiration for Jane Austen's *Mansfield Park*.

NORTHUMBERLAND
ALNWICK

The dog **Drummer**, the regimental mascot of the 1st Battalion Northumberland Fusiliers, accompanied Major Reay to South Africa at the outbreak of the Boer War and was injured in the conflict. Queen Victoria wished to give Drummer a bravery award and despite the disapproval of Parliament he was decorated.

The monument to Jerry in Wicksteed Park, Kettering.

Boer War casualty Drummer, still wearing his medals, in Alnwick Castle.

On his death he was stuffed and put on display at the regimental museum at Alnwick Castle.

The Royal Northumberland Fusiliers Museum, The Abbot's Tower, Alnwick Castle, Alnwick, Northumberland NE66 1NG. Telephone: 01665 602152. Website: www.northumberlandfusiliers.org.uk

NOTTINGHAMSHIRE
NEWSTEAD

In 1803 fifteen-year-old Lord Byron acquired **Boatswain**, a Newfoundland puppy (see page 5). He moved to Newstead Abbey in 1808, keeping a variety of pets that, with the exception of the horses, lived indoors. Forbidden to have dogs at university, he acquired a bear. Once, when swimming with Boatswain in the lake at Newstead, Byron succumbed to cramp, and the dog saved his life. In November 1808 Boatswain died of rabies. Byron erected a monument to his dog on what was believed to be the site of the high altar of the priory church. He intended to be buried there himself but was forced to sell the abbey in 1817 and so was denied this last resting place. Like many pet owners, Byron was uncomfortable with the belief that animals did not have souls, being 'Deny'd in Heaven the Soul he held on earth'. Without Boatswain to save him, Byron drowned when attempting to swim the Hellespont. Boatswain's memorial states: 'Near this spot are deposited the Remains of one who possessed Beauty without Vanity, Strength without Insolence, Courage without Ferocity and all the Virtues of Man without his Vices.

Lord Byron was saved from drowning by his dog Boatswain and had this monument built at Newstead Abbey when the dog died.

This Praise, which would be unmeaning Flattery if inscribed over human ashes, is but a just tribute to the Memory of Boatswain, a Dog who was born at Newfoundland, May 1803, and died at Newstead Abbey Nov 18th 1808.' There followed a twenty-six line poem.

Newstead Abbey Park, Ravenshead, Nottinghamshire NG15 8NA. Telephone: 01623 455900. Website: www.newsteadabbey.org.uk

RUFFORD ABBEY

Once the site of a Cistercian abbey, Rufford Abbey was owned by the Savile family until 1938. The dog graves, surrounded by iron railings, include: **Kaiser**, dog of Miss L. Savile Lumley, died 23rd August 1887; **Snuffy**, died 23rd December 1893; **Meg**, died 17th December 1909; and **Czarina**, died 13th March 1917. The grave of **Boris** bears an inscription that 'Faithful friends are hard to come by'. Many of these were working dogs.

Also buried here is **Cremorne** (1869–83), winner of the 1872 Derby and the French Grand Prix, owned by the sporting Henry Savile, who inherited the house in 1856. Being in financial difficulties, he gambled the entire estate on Cremorne winning the Derby: he won by a head. Cremorne ran in twenty-six races altogether, winning twenty, finishing second four times and third twice. A memorial statue in his honour was erected in the grounds. He was also featured on a promotional card for F. & J. Smith's cigarettes.

Rufford Country Park, Ollerton, Nottinghamshire NG22 9DF. Telephone: 0845 330 4214 or 01623 822944. Website: www.nottinghamshire.gov.uk/home/leisure/countryparks/ruffordcp.htm

Iron railings surround the graves of the Savile family's dogs at Rufford Abbey.

WELBECK

4 miles from Worksop, Welbeck Abbey Stud was founded by William John Cavendish Bentinck-Scott, Marquis of Titchfield and fifth Duke of Portland, who inherited the dukedom in 1854. The Duke constructed extensive underground tunnels and over twenty-five years employed thousands of people. He built a huge riding school with a glass roof and had about a hundred horses. A recluse and eccentric, he was rumoured to be disfigured.

Interred at Welbeck are: **Amiable**, 1891–1915; **Atalanta**, 1877–97; **Ayrshire**, 1885–1910 (his skeleton is at the Natural History Museum, South Kensington); **Carbine**, 1885–1913; **Donavon**, 1886–1905 (his hide is at Heath House, Newmarket); **Memoir**, 1887–1908; **Mowerina**, 1876–1905; **Rook**; **Semolina**, 1887–1909; **St Serf**, 1887–1915; **St Simon**, 1881–1908 (whose skeleton is at the Natural History Museum, Wollaton Hall, near Nottingham, and hide at the National Horseracing Museum at Newmarket); and **William the Third**, 1898–1917, whose skull is at the Natural History Museum in South Kensington. The park is accessible to the public.

OXFORDSHIRE
HENLEY-ON-THAMES

At the end of the Fair Mile, in front of a tree and 300 yards beyond the White Horse pub, on the south side of the road leading out of Henley towards Nettlebed, is a solitary gravestone to **Jimmy the Marmoset**. The pet of Miss Doris Jekyll, Jimmy died in 1937. They lived in New Street, Henley, in a house that is now Asquith's teddy bear shop, whose proprietors have produced a commemorative marmoset in his honour. His memorial states: 'Jimmy, a tiny marmoset. There isn't enough darkness in the world to quench the light of one small candle.'

By a busy road in Henley-on-Thames is this stone to Jimmy the marmoset.

Animal memorials at Rousham in Oxford-shire are to Ringwood, an otter hound, in the gardens (left) and to Faustina Gwynne, a cow (above), across the fields from the front of the house.

ROUSHAM

At Rousham House, built in the eighteenth century and still occupied by the Dormer family, are two long-standing animal memorials. A gravestone records the death of **Faustina Gwynne**, a Shorthorn cow who died in 1882 at the age of twenty-two, while a plaque inserted into a cascade topped by a statue of Venus commemorates **Ringwood**, an otter hound of 'extraordinary sagacity'.
Rousham House, near Steeple Aston, Oxfordshire OX25 4QX. Telephone: 01869 347110. Website: www.rousham.org

WHEATLEY

At Shotover House, in a garden made in 1718 for a friend of John Locke and Robert Boyle, twelve dogs were buried between 1913 and 1987. A stone tablet in front of the carving of a dog commemorates **Toby**, **Tim**, **Patch**, **Sammy**, **Bozz**, **Mimi**, **Pic**, **Ponpon**, **Viking**, **Tiger**, **Sherry** and **Rusty**. Shotover House, 6 miles east of Oxford on the A40, is owned by Lieutenant Colonel Sir John Miller of the Royal Scots Greys and the grounds are occasionally opened to the public under the National Gardens Scheme.

SHROPSHIRE
ACTON ROUND

At Acton Round, the home of Mr Hew Kennedy, is a memorial to **Scruffy** on a pedestal mounted by an obelisk. It bears the following inscription: 'Near this place

The obelisk to terrier Scruffy at Acton Round (left) and another to a retriever in Shirlett High Park near Much Wenlock.

lie the remains of the faithful terrier Scruffy. Severe incontinence cut short a long life at the age of 18 years, June 21 1985. If her bladder had been stronger she would have lasted even longer.'

MILLICHOPE PARK

In the beautiful eighteenth-century gardens of this Grade 2 listed building are the graves of **Bessie** and **Sassy**. The grounds were laid out in the 1760s in memory of four sons who predeceased their father.

Millichope Park. Telephone: 01584 841234.

MUCH WENLOCK

A nineteenth-century sandstone obelisk, about 15 metres high, stands at Shirlett High Park. It was apparently erected in memory of a **retriever** that fell down a mineshaft. In his will, George Forester, Squire of Willey (died 1811), instructed that upon his death his 'Aldenham horse' should be shot 'as expeditiously as possible', then buried 'with his hide on' and his grave marked by a flat stone without inscription (*Old Sports and Sportsmen* by John Randall, 1873).

TETCHILL

Born in 1939, **Rob**, a collie dog, was trained for farm work but in 1942 he was volunteered for war service. Sent to North Africa and smuggled on to a plane, he made a parachute jump, enjoying the experience so much that he underwent training. He completed twenty jumps and became the sky dog mascot for the SAS. While on the ground he acted as a guard dog, warning of the approach of enemies by licking the sleeping airmen. He also carried messages between two handlers, never allowing anyone else to intercept him. When his handlers left for Arnhem, he was not allowed on the ship. The men did not return.

Rob earned the Dickin Medal for gallantry, also the RSPCA Silver Medallion for valour. At the end of the war he was returned to Mr and Mrs Bayne of Tetchill and when he died in 1952 he was buried in the garden. His stone memorial (see page 8) states: 'To the dear memory of Rob, war dog no 471/322, twice VC, Britain's first parachute dog, who served three and a half years in North Africa and Italy with the Second Special Air Service Regiment. Died 18th January 1952 aged $12^1/_2$ years. Erected by Basil and Heather Bayne in memory of a faithful friend and playmate 1939–52.'

SOMERSET
DUNSTER

Home of the Luttrell family for six hundred years, Dunster Castle stands on an impressive wooded hill. Hidden in the trees is a dog cemetery of twenty-five graves dating from the mid twentieth century.
Dunster Castle, Dunster, near Minehead, Somerset TA24 6SL. National Trust. Telephone: 01643 821314.

ORCHARDLEIGH

Azor, a large poodle given to Thomas Swymmer Champneys by the King of Prussia in 1790, was thought to be buried beneath a monument at Wood Lodge, Orchardleigh Park. When the church was restored in 1878, however, Azor's body was discovered in the Champneys family vault. This inspired the poet Sir Henry Newbolt (1862–1938) to immortalise him in a poem 'Fidele's Grassy Tomb', dealing with the dilemma of burying an animal in consecrated ground:

> …The sum of it was that a soulless hound
> Was known to be buried in hallowed ground:
> From scandal sore the Church to save
> They must take the dog from his master's grave…

A solution was found by digging a second grave bearing the dog's name, but not containing his remains. The stone monument (see page 7) consists of a draped vase mounted on a square plinth that records how Newbolt's work 'brought Orchardleigh local literary Renown'. Newbolt and his wife were married in St Mary's church, Orchardleigh, in 1899, and both are buried there. Attractively sited on a small island, the church is now a popular venue for weddings.

STAFFORDSHIRE
ALREWAS

Among its dedications, the National Memorial Arboretum, Croxall Road, includes a memorial to members of the Civil Defence who died during the Second

The smaller of these Civil Defence memorials at the National Memorial Arboretum, Alrewas, is to 'animal friends'.

World War and also a smaller memorial to the 'Animal friends who served with such loyalty and bravery'.

BURTON UPON TRENT

Opposite the town hall are two gravestones to Staffordshire bull terrier mascots named Watchman. The name was first mentioned in 1882, when a Watchman accompanied the Staffordshire Regiment to Egypt. The tradition resumed after the Second World War when 6th Battalion The North Staffordshire Regiment (TA) was presented with **Watchman I**. He died in 1959 and the town presented **Watchman II** to the battalion in 1960. He retired in 1967, when the battalion was disbanded. The 3rd Battalion The Staffordshire Regiment was raised in 1988 and in May 1989 was presented with **Watchman III**. He died in 1998 and the battalion ceased to exist in 1999.

CANNOCK CHASE

In 1964 a weathered gravestone to **Freda**, a Dalmatian, mascot of the New Zealand Rifle Brigade, was restored at Brockton Camp. Freda died in 1918 and was buried at H Line. Four battalions of the regiment fought in France. Her collar is in the Waiourou Military Museum, New Zealand.

SHUGBOROUGH

In the grounds of the Shugborough estate, the traditional home of the Earls of Lichfield, an enigmatic cat reclines on a vase, mounted on a square plinth with goats' heads at each corner and festoons of flowers. It represents either a cat that accompanied Admiral Anson on his circumnavigation of the world or **Kouhli Khan**, a rare Persian, the last of a breed that became extinct. The monument is made

The cat monument at Shugborough.

in Coade stone. The goats on it represent the Corisan herd kept by Thomas Anson. There are also more recent stone markers to animals, such as **Spot** (1954–7), mainly gun dogs belonging to past Earls of Lichfield.
Shugborough, Milford, near Stafford ST17 0XB. National Trust. Telephone: 01889 881388. Website: www.shugborough.org.uk

STOKE-ON-TRENT
The stuffed body of a brindle whippet resides in the Potteries Museum at Stoke-on-Trent. Named for his owner, Harry Hewitt, a miner, **Hewitt's Billie** was a champion racer and rabbiter, winning the Liverpool Championship in 1914. During his career, he won his owner sufficient money to purchase his own house. Because of his success, Billie was nobbled in his last race at Latebrook, Goldenhill, in 1916, by having hard peas put between his paws. The effort of the race proved too much and he died two days later. As Harry Hewitt was then in France with the army, Billie was preserved for his return. Devoted to his pet, and despite hard times, Harry never spent the last twenty sovereigns that Billie won for him.
The Potteries Museum and Art Gallery, Bethesda Street, Hanley, Stoke-on-Trent ST1 3DW. Telephone: 01782 232323. Website: www2002.stoke.gov.uk/museums

SUFFOLK
ALDEBURGH
Snooks the dog belonged to Doctors Robin and Nora Acheson, who set up a medical practice at Aldeburgh. A commemorative statue of the dog was erected by the local people in recognition of the couple's service to the community between 1931 and 1959. Norah Acheson died in 1981 'whilst still caring'. The statue

The famous racing whippet Hewitt's Billie is in The Potteries Museum at Stoke-on-Trent.

was stolen but the original cast was found and a bronze replacement made.

NEWMARKET

Newmarket is indelibly linked with horse-racing, and there are many graves and memorials to racehorses in the neighbourhood.

Outside the National Horseracing Museum stand statues of a **Rearing Stallion** and of **Hyperion** 1930–60, who won the 1933 Derby in the record time of 2 minutes 34 seconds and also set the track record over 5 furlongs as a two-year-old. By Gainsborough out of Selene, he was small and nearly gelded as a yearling. A chestnut, he had four white feet, which was considered undesirable. He was six times champion sire, and his descendants were also successful as European show-jumpers. His articulated skeleton is at the Animal Health Trust, Lanwades Hall, Newmarket.

At Snailwell Stud on the outskirts of Newmarket is a memorial statue sculpted by John Skeating to **Chamossaire** (1943–65), winner of the St Leger, and to **Busted** (1963–88).

Nearco (1935–57), bred in Italy, won fourteen races. He stood at stud at Beech House, Newmarket, and was leading sire in 1947/8. He died aged twenty-two of cancer, and his grave at

Above: *Snooks is a popular attraction on the seafront at Aldeburgh, just south of the Moot Hall.*

Left: *Hyperion stands just outside the National Horseracing Museum in Newmarket, which has a fine permanent collection reflecting the history and drama of the turf.*

The plinth of this statue of Mill Reef bears a history of his achievement. It is on show at the National Stud, Newmarket.

the stud is marked by a stone book.

St Paddy (1957–84), who won the 1960 St Leger, is likewise buried at Beech House.

Owen Tudor (1938–66) and **Abernant** (1946–70) were father and son. Owen Tudor won fourteen of his seventeen races. Both are buried at the Egerton Stud, their graves marked by matching stones.

Mill Reef (1968–86), who won the 1971 Derby, 2,000 Guineas and Eclipse Stakes, is commemorated at the National Stud. He suffered devastating damage to a leg but was able to stand at stud. His statue was designed by John Skeaping, bearing the words spoken by Paul Mellon at the 1970 Gimcrack Dinner.

> Swift as a bird I flew down many a course.
> Princes, Lords, Commoners all sang my praise.
> In victory or defeat I played my part.
> Remember me, all men who love the horse,
> If hearts and spirits flag in other days,
> Though small, I gave my all, I gave my heart

Other stallions remembered at the National Stud are Air Express, Blakeney, Moorestyle, Never Say Die, Relkino and Tudor Melody.

Two stallions buried at Lanwades Hall are **Jeddah** (1895–1909), winner of the 1898 Derby, and **Ninisky**, successful stallion at the former stud. Lanwades Hall is now part of the Animal Health Trust.

National Horseracing Museum, 99 High Street, Newmarket, Suffolk CB8 8JL. Telephone: 01638 667333. Website: www.nhrm.co.uk

National Stud, Newmarket, Suffolk CB8 0XE. Telephone: 01638 663464. Website: www.nationalstud.co.uk

THORNHAM MAGNA

Graves and memorials to horses, dogs and cats feature prominently in the grounds of Thornham Walks. Numerous pet dogs of the Henniker family are remembered on a joint monument to 'faithful dogs' recalled with the caption: 'He prayeth best who loveth best with man and bird and beast.'

A separate dog memorial to 'faithful dogs of Arthur and Florence Henniker' commemorates **Small, Fan, Watch, Rattler** and **Chevy**. The dedication reads:

There are men both good and wise
Who hold that in future state
Dumb creatures we have cherished here below
Will give us joyous greeting
When we pass the golden gate
Is it folly that I hope it may be so.
Whyte Melville

Floyd (1972–87), a black cat, and **Mutlu** are remembered, complete with a cat carving, but perhaps more sombre are the memorial stones erected in the grounds to horses: **Mahuta**, who served with the Coldstream Guards in Egypt in 1882 at the Battle of Tel-el-Kebir and retired on a pension to Thornham, where he died in 1886; **Joll** and **Punch**, both of whom were born and died at Thornham; **Ioto**, who served in South Africa, was wounded at Magersfontein and killed at Pretoria in 1900; and **Nulli Secundus 'Bob'**, the Adjutant's charger with the Coldstream Guards in the Egyptian

Thornham Walks, with its restored walled garden and Gothic folly, has a pets' cemetery renovated in 1999 to commemorate the sixth Lord Henniker.

One of the many animal graves at Silvermere Cemetery, Cobham, is this of an alligator.

Campaign, 1882, who died at Thornham aged seventeen years. His monument was erected by Major Henniker in 1895.

Thornham Walks, Red House Yard, Thornham Magna, Eye, Suffolk IP23 8HH. Telephone: 01379 788345. Website: www.thornhamfieldcentre.org

SURREY
COBHAM

Opened in 1977, Silvermere Cemetery in Byfleet Road is one of the biggest animal cemeteries in Britain, with over two thousand burials. These include Monty the alligator, a python, and a dog and a rabbit sharing a coffin.

EPSOM

The Durdans in Chalk Lane was the home of the first Duke of Cumberland and later of the fifth Earl of Rosebery. It has long been associated with horse-racing. In 1838 Sir G. Heathcote's **Amato** had his single success in winning the Derby. The local pub was named in his honour. He died in 1841 and was buried in a grave surrounded by ornamental railings beneath a stone slab incised with his name.

Five horses belonging to Lord Rosebery were also buried in the grounds: **Ladas** (1891–1914), who won the 1894 Derby; **Sir Visto** (1892–1914), who won the Derby in 1895 and the St Leger; **Cicero** (1902–22), who won the 1905 Derby; **Illuminata**, who was dam of Cicero and Ladas; **Velasquez (**1894).

Private residence.

The grave of Derby winner Amato at The Durdans, Epsom.

Evocation of Speed, a fine bronze sculpture on a steel plinth by Judy Boyt, marks the achievements of **Diomed** (1777–1808), who won the first ever Derby in 1780, and the winner in 2000, **Galileo**. Diomed is said to be buried in Virginia on the property of Colonel Hoomes, Bowling Green. *Evocation of Speed* won the British Sporting Art Trust award in 2001 and is sited at the Derby Square, the Ebbisham Centre, Epsom. It was commissioned by Epsom and Ewell Borough Council.

GUILDFORD

Statues of **Alice and the White Rabbit** stand in the park at Mill Mead, Guildford. Lewis Carroll often stayed with his sisters, who lived in the town.

KINGSTON UPON THAMES

In 1895, while living with his original owner's widow, **Nipper**, the HMV dog, died aged eleven years. He was buried beneath a mulberry tree in Eden Street. Fifty-four years later, the Gramophone Company honoured his memory by erecting a plaque but the site was later taken over by Lloyds Bank and Nipper's grave was buried beneath the car park. In 1984 two plaques were unveiled at the bank by the chairman of HMV shops, one inside and one on the wall outside. Nipper is also commemorated at Bristol (*qv*).

POLESDEN LACEY

Eighteen graves at Polesden Lacey, bearing details of dogs' dates and breed on identical stones, mark the burial places of Margaret Greville's pets. They include **Dougal**, a West Highlander, died 1938; **Caesar**, an Airedale; and **Tyne**, a collie. Other dogs include white collies, Japanese spaniels, Pekinese, cairn terriers and a retriever.
Polesden Lacey, Great Bookham, near Dorking, Surrey RH5 6BD. National Trust. Telephone: 01372 452048.

The dogs' burial ground at the National Trust's property Polesden Lacey is immaculately kept.

THAMES DITTON

Three police horses were awarded the Dickin Medal for courage during the Second World War.

In April 1941 **Regal** showed amazing bravery when the forage room at Muswell Hill caught fire after an incendiary bomb fell nearby. Alone in the stable, he did not panic. In 1944 he again risked injury and braved the effects of falling debris when fire followed an attack.

Olga quite naturally bolted when four houses collapsed near her at Tooting but she returned to the scene of devastation to carry out traffic control duties and assisted in rescue operations. **Upstart** showed no fear when a bomb exploded at Bethnal Green. He was showered with glass and debris but carried on with the job of traffic control.

All three horses received awards on 11th April 1947 and their medals are held at the museum of the Metropolitan Police Mounted Training Establishment, Thames Ditton.

Winston became famous as the mount ridden by the young Queen Elizabeth II during Trooping the Colour. He died of a broken back when collapsing in the street at Thames Ditton. A square stone bearing his name is just inside the gate at the Establishment.

Quicksilver was the mount of Colonel Percy Lawrie, Assistant Police Commissioner, who served in the First World War. Quicksilver received three medals: the War Medal, the Victory Medal and the Defence Medal.

WEYBRIDGE

Once the site of a Tudor palace, Oatlands Park was acquired by Henry VIII in 1538 as a home for Anne of Cleves but she never lived there. Prince Rupert, Charles I's nephew, made it his headquarters during the Civil War and in 1650 the old palace was pulled down. In 1790 the Duke of York, second son of George III, took up residence with his Duchess, Frederica, daughter of the King of Prussia. Passionate about animals and often alone, the Duchess acquired many dogs. When a fire broke out, she risked her life to rescue them. Fifty were buried in the grounds. Many headstones are now placed along the terrace. A map of the cemetery and a gravestone to a pet named **Billey** are in Weybridge Museum.

A statue of the Duchess is on Monument Green at Weybridge. She died in 1820.

Oatlands is now a hotel. Oatlands Park Hotel, Oatlands Drive, Weybridge, Surrey KT13 9HB. Telephone: 01932 847242. Website: www.oatlandsparkhotel.co.uk

The headstones of Frederica, Duchess of York's many pets are kept in an enclosure at Oatlands Park Hotel, Weybridge.

SUSSEX
BRIGHTON

In a walled garden behind Preston Manor is a well-maintained and peaceful **pet cemetery**. Created by Ellen Thomas, a keen dog owner, it has been used as a burial place for animals employed by the council. The present garden, laid out to a seventeenth-century design, dates from 1905 and is open to the public on weekdays.
Preston Manor, Preston Drove, Brighton, East Sussex BN1 6SD. Telephone: 01273 292770. Website: www.prestonmanor.virtualmuseum.info

BURWASH

In the grounds of Bateman's, the home of Rudyard Kipling, are four headstones to dogs belonging to the writer. Only those to **Mop** and **Kate** are now legible. Other dogs Kipling owned include **Jack, Betty (Bet), Rollo, Togo** and **Worry**, some of whom are known to have been West Highland or Scottish terriers. The characters of his dogs were illustrated in Kipling's letters to his children, published in a book called *O Beloved Kids*, collated by Elliot L. Gilbert.
Bateman's, Burwash, Etchingham, East Sussex TN19 7DS. National Trust. Telephone: 01435 882302.

RYE

Headstones on the wall of Lamb House commemorate **Nick, June**, **Peter, Tosca**, **Tim** and **Taffy**. Once the home of Henry James, Lamb House in West Street is administered by the National Trust.
Lamb House, West Street, Rye, East Sussex TN31 7ES. National Trust. Telephone: 01372 453401.

WORTHING

In the grounds of Beach Park stands a fountain surrounded by flowerbeds,

In Worthing's Beach Park colourful flower beds surround a fountain dedicated to pigeons that died on war service.

erected in the memory of **pigeons who died in war**. It was donated by Nancy Price and the People's Theatre, London. Bearing the message: 'Birds of the air shall carry the voice and that which hath wings shall tell the matter. This memorial is presented by Nancy Price and members of the People's Theatre, London.' There is also a plaque stating: 'On top of this mound is a memorial to warrior birds who gave their lives on active service 1939–45. It is also for the pleasure and use of living birds.'

During the Second World War 200,000 pigeons were donated by fanciers to the war effort. Thirty-two pigeons were awarded the Dickin Medal for acts of gallantry. Among the most famous was **G I Joe**, who, flying 20 miles in twenty minutes, carried a message to abort a bombing campaign that would have killed over a thousand British soldiers. Joe was awarded his medal by the Lord Mayor of London. He is displayed in the Historical Centre, Meyer Hall, Fort Monmouth, New Jersey, USA.

Others include: **Winkie**, who crashed with her plane but, although oiled, made it to land to get help; **Ruhr Express**, who carried out three hundred missions and flew in record time; **Gustav**, the first to deliver a message from the Normandy beaches; **William of Orange**, who covered 260 miles, mostly over water, in 4 hours and 25 minutes; **White Vision**, who travelled 60 miles over rough seas and in poor visibility when her ship foundered around the Hebrides; **Maquis,** who three times brought important messages from France; **Mary of Exeter**, who received her medal for 'Outstanding endurance on War Service in spite of wounds'. She is buried in the PDSA cemetery at Ilford, her grave marked by a headstone.

Cher Ami flew twelve successful missions during the First World War. His last was to take a message from a band of American servicemen trapped behind enemy lines. By pinpointing their position they avoided bombardment by their own men and many lives were saved. In the mission, Cher Ami was badly wounded, losing a leg. The French honoured him with a Croix de Guerre. Cher Ami died within the year but is on display at the Smithsonian Institute, Washington DC.

There are also memorials in Belgium and in northern France (Lille) to twenty thousand pigeons who died in the war.

WILTSHIRE
CASTLE COMBE

In the grounds of the Manor House Hotel, beneath the statue of a young man with a dog, are incised the names of **Wallace**, died November 1880, **Crab**, died February 1884, and **Peter** (a cat), who was buried in September 1884. Their owners are long since forgotten.

SALISBURY

Adopted by Sergeant Kelly of the 66th Berkshire Regiment when serving in Malta, **Bobbie** accompanied him to Afghanistan and was wounded at the Battle of Maiwand in 1880. After the regiment returned to Browndown Barracks, Gosport, Bobbie was presented to Queen Victoria at Osborne House, along with the men. Shortly afterwards, Bobbie was run over by a hansom cab. A commemorative stone placed at the barracks seems to have disappeared but Bobbie herself was stuffed and is displayed at the Royal Gloucestershire, Berkshire and Wiltshire Regiment Museum at The Wardrobe, Salisbury.

The Wardrobe, The Royal Gloucestershire, Berkshire and Wiltshire Regiment Museum, 58 The Close, Salisbury, Wiltshire SP1 2EX. Telephone: 01722 419419. Website: www.thewardrobe.org.uk

One of the few survivors of the Battle of Maiwand in 1880 during the Second Afghan War, Bobbie is now on show at the Royal Gloucestershire, Berkshire and Wiltshire Regiment Museum in Salisbury.

SWINDON

Between 1905 and 1914 **Bruce**, a St Bernard, was a significant figure around Swindon collecting money for the hospital. Famously, he barked a 'thank you' for each coin placed in his box. Belonging to Mr T. Beale of Nelson Street, he was buried in the back yard but his grave is no longer identified. His collar and collecting box were donated to the Swindon Museum and a postcard was made stating that he belonged to the Brotherhood of Hero Dogs, London.

WORCESTERSHIRE
LOWER BROADHEATH

Marco, a spaniel, and **Mina**, a Cairn terrier, were the pets of Edward Elgar. His wife hated dogs and until she died Elgar's pets were boarded with his sister. As a puppy, Marco was taken ill and Elgar cancelled his London musical engagements to look after him. Marco outlived his master by five years. Elgar commemorated Mina in his last complete orchestral work, called simply *Mina*. Both dogs had places laid at the dinner table, hopefully being better behaved than Thomas Hardy's

The gravestone of Sir Edward Elgar's dogs Marco and Mina, at the Elgar Birthplace in Worcestershire.

Wessex. In the *Enigma Variations*, Elgar portrayed Dan, the bulldog belonging to G. R. Sinclair, the Hereford organist, paddling in the water.

When the First World War broke out Elgar was distressed at the thought of animals suffering. In a letter to his friend Frank Schuster he wrote: 'The only thing that wrings my heart and soul is the thought of the horses – Oh! My beloved animals. The men and women can go to hell – but the horses...'

Elgar died in 1934. Marco and Mina are buried at the Elgar Birthplace museum, Lower Broadheath, Worcester, opened by his daughter Carice.

Elgar Birthplace, Crown East Lane, Lower Broadheath, Worcestershire WR2 6RH. Telephone: 01905 333224. Website: www.elgarfoundation.org

WORCESTER

Carved into the wall of Worcester Cathedral by the Water Gate is the outline of a huge **sturgeon** taken from the River Severn in 1835. It measured 94 inches and the actual fish is on display in the museum in Foregate Street.

YORKSHIRE
MIDDLEHAM

The grave of **Pretender,** winner of the 1869 Derby and the 2,000 Guineas, is marked by a huge stone at Brecongill Stud. Pretender is said to have been buried standing beneath it.

SKIPTON

An obelisk bearing the names of **Tatters** (June 1918 to September 1928) and **Spotty** (October 1913 to December 1928) stands in the grounds of Broughton Hall, home of the Tempest family since 1594.

The house is run as a business park but the grounds are open to the public.

Broughton Hall, Skipton, North Yorkshire BD23 3AE. Telephone: 01756 799608. Website: www.broughtonhall.co.uk

YORK

Polly, a parrot, and **Rough**, a dog, belonged to Frank Green of the Treasurer's House. Rough's grave is in the garden. Green, grandson of an ambitious engineer, owned the house from 1897 until 1930, when he gave it to the National Trust, the first house to be donated. A portrait of another dog, **Frisk**, hangs in the house.

Treasurer's House, Minster Yard, York YO1 7JL. National Trust. Telephone: 01904 624247.

Among the steam engines and railway memorabilia at the National Railway Museum is a stuffed Airedale in a glass case. This is **Laddie**, who was born in 1948 and acted as a collecting dog on behalf of a railway charity, the Southern Railwaymen's Home for Old People, working mainly at Waterloo station in London. On retiring from this work, he went to live at the home in Woking, Surrey, until he died in 1960. He was then stuffed and put in a glass case, to continue his collecting work, at Wimbledon station. In 1990 he moved to the National Railway Museum, where he still serves the same purpose.

National Railway Museum, Leeman Road, York YO26 4XJ. Telephone: 01904 621261. Website: www.nrm.org.uk

John McKenna's Jersey cows are a delightful tourist attraction in St Helier.

CHANNEL ISLANDS

JERSEY

In 2001, to honour the famous **Jersey cows,** a memorial group was unveiled at West's Centre, St Helier. The monument was created by the Scottish sculptor John McKenna.

SCOTLAND

CRIEFF

The Famous Grouse distillery erected a bronze statue to its celebrated employee, **Towser** the cat. Towser disposed of thirty thousand rodents during his twenty-four year career as the distillery's mouser, a unique achievement as recorded in the *Guinness Book of Records*. He may have been helped by a nightly 'nip' in his milk. A cat protection charity was asked to find a replacement and two cats, Dylan and Brooke, were employed – Towser being a hard act to follow.

EDINBURGH

Sigmund Neuberger, 'the Great Lafayette' (1871–1911), an illusionist and conjurer, was the highest-paid entertainer of his time. His act included pigeons, a lion, horses, a turkey and a small child who was made to disappear and reappear. It also included **Beauty**, a dog on whom Neuberger doted. So attached to her was he that she had her own bathroom and shared Lafayette's suite when on tour. Her effigy

Towser of The Famous Grouse Distillery was commemorated for his record-breaking war on vermin. Helen Ralston of Cats Protection pats his statue.

appeared on the radiator of his car and his Credit Lyonnais cheques bore a picture of her sitting up and begging beside two bags of gold, with the words 'My two best friends'. Beauty wore a silvered and bejewelled collar given to Neuberger in 1899 by Harry Houdini.

In May 1911 Lafayette started a two-week engagement at the Empire Palace Theatre, Nicholson Street, Edinburgh, but on 4th May Beauty died. Distraught, Lafayette arranged for her embalming and burial at Piershill Cemetery, Portobello Road. This was agreed to only when he bought a plot in which to be buried himself. The funeral was arranged for 10th May. However, on 9th May, as the illusion 'The Lion's Bride' was being performed, a curtain caught fire. Fortunately the audience of three thousand all escaped but eight members of the troupe, including Lafayette himself, and the horse and the lion were killed. It was believed that Lafayette might have escaped

In Piershill Cemetery, Edinburgh, the ashes of the Great Lafayette share a grave with his dog Beauty.

had he not turned back to save his horse.

Lafayette's cremated body was buried on Sunday 14th May. Some sixty coaches followed the procession. He and Beauty share the grave.

In Greyfriars Churchyard, Candlemaker Row, stands a statue and memorial to **Bobby**, a Skye terrier who stayed for fourteen years at the grave of his dead master, John Gray, a policeman (some say a farmer), who died in 1858 (see page 6). Bobby returned nightly to the cemetery until the curator, James Brown, took pity on him. The dog would not leave the vicinity of the grave even in the worst weather and because of his loyalty he was given a collar by the Lord Provost of Edinburgh, who paid for his dog licence. Bobby died in 1872 and was buried in the churchyard. He was modelled from life by William Brodie, who sculpted a shallow fountain with a column on which Bobby was mounted. A memorial plaque was erected by the Dog Aid Society of Scotland and unveiled by the Duke of Gloucester in 1981. It bears the dedication: 'Let his loyalty and devotion be a lesson to us all.' On the wall above number 34 Candlemaker Row, there is a sign in a gilded frame, depicting a seated dog in profile.

The regimental mascot of the 1st Battalion Scots Guards from 1853 to 1860, **Bob** originally belonged to a butcher in Windsor but deserted him for the regiment, sailing with them to the Crimea and nearly being lost when he boarded the wrong ship. He was present at the

The gravestone of Greyfriars Bobby in Greyfriars Churchyard.

battles of Balaclava, Inkerman and Sebastopol, and at the Alma he was listed as missing, but turned up again. At Inkerman he chased cannonballs and was rewarded with a medal. After returning to Britain he met a sad end under the wheels of a butcher's cart. He is now on display at the National War Museum of Scotland.

National War Museum of Scotland, Edinburgh Castle, Edinburgh EH1 2NG. Telephone: 0131 247 4413. Website: www.nms.ac.uk

Khan, a German shepherd dog, belonging to the Railton family of Tolworth, Surrey, was volunteered for war service and seconded to the 6th Battalion Cameronians based in Lanarkshire. Khan and his handler, Corporal Jimmy Muldoon, soon became inseparable.

In 1944 they were sent to the Dutch Island of Walcheren to dislodge the occupying German force. A detachment was sent by boat, landing on the mud banks. Khan swam ashore but, amid the gunfire, he lost Muldoon, who was unable to swim. He returned to the water and, 200 yards out, found his friend. Muldoon held on to the dog's collar as Khan swam ashore, thereby saving the soldier's life. For this act, he was awarded the Dickin Medal on 27th March 1945. The citation reads: 'For rescuing Corporal Muldoon from drowning under heavy shell fire at the assault of Walcheron, November 1944, while serving with the 6th Cameronians.'

Understandably, Muldoon wished to keep Khan but after the war he was returned to his owners. At a parade of war dogs, when the two met again, their mutual joy was so obvious it was agreed that Khan should return with his handler. They were regarded as celebrities and given the freedom of Lanark.

Khan is believed to be buried in the animals' cemetery at Edinburgh Castle. Two graves bear the inscription 'Cameronians' Dog'.

Historic Scotland has identified twenty-six burials or memorials to animals in Edinburgh Castle, dating back to the 1840s. Among these are **Jess**, band pet of the 42nd Royal Highlanders, died 1881; **Gyp**, the Crown Room dog, died 1911; and the most recent, **Bendicks**, pet of the Governor of the Castle, 1998.
Edinburgh Castle, Edinburgh. Telephone: 0131 225 9846. Website: www.historic-scotland.gov.uk

GLAMIS
Pets belonging to Elizabeth Bowes Lyon at Glamis Castle, the ancestral home of the Earls of Strathclyde, include **Fizz Whizzy** (1961–75), **Johnny** (1972–7), **Puffin** (1967–82) and **Happy**, a guinea-pig (1993–1997).

GLASGOW
Wallace the Fire Dog first appeared in 1894 when he attached himself to a city fire engine at a lifeboat procession, following it back to the fire station. His owner collected him but he returned to the station and took up residence. Eventually the corporation paid for his dog licence.

When the brigade was called out, Wallace was always ahead of the horse-drawn appliances, seeming to know where the incident was. It seems the driver would indicate the direction with his whip and Wallace followed the signals with an occasional glance over his shoulder. Once, when Wallace was suffering from a sore paw, a local resident had rubber shoes made for him.

When Wallace died in 1902 his body was embalmed and placed in the Central Fire Station. When the station closed, Wallace was transferred to the Central Command Headquarters at Cowcaddens, Glasgow.

KINMOUNT
On the Kinmount Estate, once the seat of the Marquises of Queensberry, is a neglected headstone to **Chong,** died 17th February 1932 aged eleven years, 'An old Friend'.

LANARK
The owner of Vere House, Lanark, believing that his neighbour had poisoned his dog, is said to have placed a statue where it could be seen from the neighbouring house as a stark reminder.

The 'Moffat Ram' in the centre of this Scottish town celebrates the black-faced sheep that are a feature of the local countryside.

MOFFAT

The **Colvin Monument,** also referred to as the 'Moffat Ram', is a black-faced sheep atop a drinking fountain, presented to Moffat by William Colvin, a Lanarkshire ironmaster. It was intended to provide pure drinking water although the lead pipes brought their own hazards. The sculptor was listed as Mr Brodie of Edinburgh. When it was observed that the ram had no ears, the ridicule allegedly drove the sculptor to commit suicide. On the base it states: 'A gift to the town of Moffat from William Colvin of Craigielands 1875'.

MONREITH

At Monreith on Luce Bay a bronze sculpture of **Mijbil**, a pet otter, forms a fitting tribute to the writer Gavin Maxwell. Mijbil was brought back from southern Iraq, where Maxwell had spent time with the Marsh Arabs, and the story of his time in the western Highlands is told in the book and subsequent film, *Ring of Bright Water*. Mijbil was killed by an otter hunter for his pelt. Gavin Maxwell died in 1969.

NEWHAILES

Newhailes House, dating from the seventeenth and eighteenth centuries and visited by Samuel Johnson, was owned by Sir David Dalrymple, a member of a Scottish

Mijbil, Gavin Maxwell's pet otter, commemorates the author at Monreith.

At Newhailes House local residents have created a cemetery for their own pets.

legal and political family. **Tam, Bobo, Bobby** and **Fred** are buried in the grounds. In 1997 the property was donated to the Scottish National Trust.
Newhailes House, Newhailes Road, Musselburgh, East Lothian EH21 6RY. National Trust for Scotland. Telephone: 0131 653 5599. Website: www.nts.org.uk

PENICUIK

Penicuik House, built in 1761, was designed by the owner, Sir John Clerk MP (1684–1755), politician and patron of the arts, who also planned nearby Penicuik village. Graves of **Kitty, Dash** and other pets are marked by posts in the grounds. The house remains in the Clerk family and is occasionally open to the public under the National Gardens Scheme.

WALES

ABERGAVENNY

Foxhunter, a famous show-jumper ridden by Harry Llewellyn in the 1950s, is buried in the Foxhunter Car Park for the Blorenge Mountain near Abergavenny (see page 4). A memorial plaque states: '3rd April 1940 – 21st November 1959. Here lies Foxhunter, champion international show jumper, winner of 78 international competitions including many foreign Grand Prix and the George VI Gold Cup 1948, 1950 and 1953. 35 times member of the British show jumping team which won Olympic gold medal at Helsinki 1952, bronze medals at London 1948, Prince of Wales Cup, London 5 times (1949–53) and the Aga Khan Cup outright, Dublin (1950, 1951–1953).'

ABERYSTWYTH

At Nanteos House near Aberystwyth, which was owned by the Jones family and their successors through marriage until 1951, twenty-three graves record the passing of family pets. The death of **Traveller**, 'a favourite retriever', acknowledges: 'that undiscovered Country from whose bourne no traveller returns'. More curious are the graves of **Poor Jack the Coon and his wife**. It has been suggested that they may have been slaves but the grave predates the introduction of this derogatory word. As wild animals were kept as pets, they might possibly have been racoons, but as the Welsh word for dogs is *cyn*, it is more likely that the epitaph was a phonetic mis-spelling by a non-Welsh-speaking mason. Nanteos is now a language school.

BANGOR

Buried at Penrhyn Castle, Bangor, are **Pandy, Suzette, Wanda** and **Pepper**, believed to have been pugs, belonging to the Douglas Pennant family. They were buried during the 1920s and 1930s.
Penrhyn Castle, Bangor, Gwynedd LL57 4HN. National Trust. Telephone: 01248 353084.

BEDDGELERT

Near to the Royal Goat Hotel, Beddgelert, are commemorative stones and slate tablets to **Gelert**. The grave was erected in 1802 by David Pritchard, owner of the hotel, in an attempt to attract visitors. The tablets, in Welsh and English, state: 'In the 13th century, Llewelyn, Prince of North Wales, had a palace at Beddgelert. One day he went hunting without Gelert, "the faithful hound", who was unaccountably absent on Llewelyn's return. The truant, stained and smeared with blood, joyfully sprang to meet his master. The prince, alarmed, hastened to his son and saw the infant's cot empty, the bedclothes and floor covered with blood. The frantic father plunged his sword into the hound's side, thinking he had killed his heir. The dog's dying yell was answered by a child's cry. Llewelyn searched and discovered his boy unharmed but nearby lay the body of a mighty wolf which Gelert had slain. The prince, filled with remorse, is said never to have smiled again. He buried Gelert. The spot is called Beddgelert.'

CARDIFF

In 1997 a sculpture of **Billy the Seal** by David Petersen was unveiled by the Lord Mayor of Cardiff to mark the centenary of Victoria Park. The two accompanying commemorative slate slabs are inscribed in Welsh and English. Billy was resident in the park from 1912 to 1939, having been caught in a fishing net. Over the years several mates were found for Billy, but none of them lived for long. On his death he was discovered to be a female. In the floods of 1927 she left the confines of the park and was found swimming down the road.

CARDIGAN

A stone sculpture of the **Teifi Otter** by Geoffrey Powell was erected at the Prince Charles Quay, Cardigan, to mark the golden jubilee of the Dyfed Wildlife Trust. It was unveiled by David Bellamy.

CHIRK

There are approximately nine graves, including headstones to **Grip** and other dogs, in the grounds of Chirk Castle. Although the stones are eroded and difficult to see, the pets are 'much lamented'.

Chirk Castle was occupied for nearly seven hundred years, latterly in the hands

Billy the Seal was a popular attraction at Victoria Park in Cardiff between the two World Wars.

of the Myddleton family, who still hold some of the estate.
Chirk Castle, Chirk, Wrexham LL14 5AF. National Trust. Telephone: 01691 777701.

CILIAU AERON
 A slate slab set in three rows in the woodland around the lake at Llanerchaeron commemorates **Vic**, a dog that died on 26th June 1919 aged thirteen years.
Llanerchaeron, Ciliau Aeron, near Aberaeron, Ceredigion SA48 8DG. National Trust. Telephone: 01545 570200.

LLANDUDNO
 At the Bodysgallen Hotel is a grave to **Funny**, a dog belonging to Mrs Frances Mostyn. Her dedication says: 'Mrs Frances Mostyn's faithful Funny, died April 1820 aged about ten years. She was the most attached, most intelligent and interesting of four-footed friends. This home is a monument to your love.'
 Jasper (1981–94) belonged to an owner of the hotel, who left his grave to be attended by future proprietors. The inscription remembers 'A true friend of noble countenance and most affectionate nature'.

 On the promenade at Llandudno is a memorial to Lewis Carroll's **White Rabbit,** unveiled in 1933. Lewis Carroll was a frequent visitor to Llandudno, where he stayed with Dean Liddell and his family, including his daughter Alice. The memorial was commissioned by the Alice in Wonderland Society, sculpted by F. W. Forrester, and unveiled by David Lloyd George. A protective cage was added in 1988. The inscription on the pedestal reads: 'On this very shore during happy rambles with little Alice Liddell Lewis Carroll was inspired to write that literary treasure *Alice in Wonderland*, which has charmed children for generations. Unveiled by the Rt Hon D. Lloyd George OM, MP, Sept 6th 1933.'

Gravestones a hundred and seventy years apart at Bodysgallen Hotel, Llandudno.

NEWPORT

Buried at Tredegar House, the former home of Lord Tredegar near Newport, is **Peeps**, a Skye terrier. The inscription on his tomb reads: 'In loving memory of Peeps, fondest and most affectionate of Skye terriers, who died Sept 6th 1898. "His honest heart was all his master's own". There are some both good and wise who say dumb creatures we have cherished here below shall give us joyous greeting when we reach the golden gate. Is it folly that I hope it may be so?'

Two other dogs, **Friday** and **Barry**, are buried in the grounds.

Sir Briggs, the horse ridden by Lord Tredegar in the Charge of the Light Brigade, has a memorial in the Cedar Garden. The dedication states: 'In memory of Sir Briggs, a favourite charger. He carried his master, the Hon Godfrey Morgan, Captain 17th Lancers, boldly and well at the Battle of the Alma, in the first line in the light cavalry charge of Balaclava, and at the Battle of Inkerman 1854. He died at Tredegar Park Feb 8th 1974 aged 28 years.'

In 1909 an equestrian statue of Lord Tredegar and Sir Briggs was erected in Cardiff city centre. It stands in front of the National Museum of Wales.

Tredegar House and Park, 2 miles west of Newport, are run by Newport Council. The grounds are open all year round.
Tredegar House and Park, Newport NP1 9YW. Telephone: 01633 815880.
Website: www.newport.gov.uk

The obelisk at Tredegar House, Newport, to Sir Briggs, ridden in the famous Charge of the Light Brigade.

One of the stones at the cemetery in Portmeirion.

ROGER
1984 - 1998
OUR DEAR LOVING FRIEND
WHO LOVED THESE WOODS.
HIS BRIGHT SPIRIT
WILL BE SADLY MISSED.

PORTMEIRION

At Portmeirion, the village created between 1925 and 1975 by Clough Williams-Ellis, is a dogs' graveyard established by Mrs Adelaide Haig, who lived in the mansion from 1870 to 1917. Her assorted dogs lived in the Mirror Room in the house, where she read sermons to them. The headstones are of black marble and the cemetery is still in use.

Portmeirion, Gwynedd LL48 6ET. Telephone: 01766 770000. Website: www.portmeirion-village.com

TREGARON

A sad end met the **Tregaron elephant**, travelling with a menagerie around 1900. North of Tregaron were some of the largest lead-mining works in the world and the elephant is believed to have died from drinking polluted water. He is thought to be buried in the Talbot Gardens, where a huge stone marks the spot.

NORTHERN IRELAND

MOUNT STEWART

In the grounds of Mount Stewart, Newtownards, nominated as a World Heritage site, there are dog burials and memorials to horses near the lake. There is also a plaque to **Macky**, a cockatoo.

Mount Stewart House, Portaferry Road, Newtownards, County Down BT22 2AD. National Trust. Telephone: 028 4278 8387.

THE ARGORY

Once home of the Bond family, The Argory has a grave to **Vic**, a dog who died on 9th September 1909. Vic belonged to Captain Shelton, who survived the sinking of the *Birkenhead*, the first occasion on which the procedure of evacuating women and children before men from a sinking ship was adopted. It became known as the Birkenhead Drill.

The Argory, 144 Derrycaw Road, Moy, Dungannon, County Armagh BT71 6NA. National Trust. Telephone: 028 8778 4753.

REPUBLIC OF IRELAND

DUBLIN

At the entrance to the Casino at Marino, mounted on a granite plinth, is a monument to **Nep (Neptune)**, a black Labrador, pet of the children of the second Lord Charlemont, Francis Caulfield. Anne Bermingham, his wife, was said to have been much admired by Lord Byron and the words on the tablet are believed to have been penned by him.

> Beneath, where Lilies raise their tiny crests,
> All that remains of faithful Neptune rests.
> Nor, Stranger, scoff, if o'er his humble bier,

A Master's eye has shed affection's tear;
It is for Man to scan the ways of Heav'n
And, proudly boast, to him alone, are giv'n
Those noblest emanations from above,
Truth, Honesty, Fidelity, and Love;
If such emotions in thy bosom swell,
My Noble Dog possess'd them all as well,
Courage was his, in danger to defend,
Promptness to search each look, each nod attend,
Patience for hours, to brave e'en Winter's gale,
With bounding Joy, a lov'd approach to hail,
Impulsive Bound whose ev'ry action show'd
A Heart within, where fond attachment glow'd.
Faithful and True, in gentleness, a Child,
His Death was placid, as his Life was mild.
Advanced in Years, in sorrow, rarely tried,
He calmly sank upon the grass and Died.

DUNGARVAN

The life of **Master McGrath,** champion greyhound and three times winner of the Waterloo Cup, was surrounded by mystery. Belonging to Lord Lurgan, although bred and 'owned' by James Galwey-Foley, Master McGrath died in 1871. Rumours abounded that he had been poisoned. Others said his heart succumbed to the strain of racing and he was believed to have been doped on the only occasion he was defeated. Known as the Great Black and commemorated in song, he was so famous that Queen Victoria asked for him to be presented at court. A life-size statue was erected at Pennington House near Lymington in Hampshire but was taken by Lord Lurgan's godson to Ireland. A statue also stands outside Dungarvan at the junction of Cappoquin Road and the Clonmel Road. The name of the sculptor is unknown, as is the last resting place of Master McGrath. In 1873 Lord Lurgan presented Queen Victoria with a greyhound bitch, Giddy.

POWERSCOURT

Powerscourt, Enniskerry, houses one of the largest private pet cemeteries in an Irish garden, containing pets belonging to the Wingfield and Slazenger families. They include cats, dogs and **Princess**, an Aberdeen Angus cow who died in 1972 aged eleven years, having been three times Dublin champion. The most famous resident was probably **Eugenie**, a Jersey cow who produced seventeen calves and over 100,000 gallons of milk. She died in 1967.

Powerscourt, Enniskerry, Bray, County Wicklow. Telephone: +353 (1) 204 6000. Website: www.powerscourt.org/gardens

Further reading

Cooper, Jilly. *Animals in War*. Corgi, 1984.
Lambton, Lucinda. *Beastly Buildings: Architecture for Animals*. Jonathan Cape, 1985.
Leith, Sam. *Dead Pets: Stuff Them, Eat Them, Love Them*. Canongate Books, 2005.
MacDonagh, Katherine. *Reigning Cats and Dogs*. Fourth Estate, 1999.
Mottistone, Lord (Colonel Jack Seely). *My Horse Warrior*. Hodder & Stoughton 1834.
Orrell, Bob, and Vincent, Margaret. *Some Lakeland Monuments*. Bob Orrell Publications, undated.

Further information

Pet burials

For information and membership of the Association of Private Pet Cemeteries and Crematoria, contact: Nunclose, Armathwaite, Carlisle, Cumbria CA4 9JT; telephone: 01252 844478; website: www.appcc.org.uk.

Details of properties mentioned in the gazetter, and owned by either the National Trust or English Heritage can be found on their respective websites:
www.nationaltrust.org.uk
www.english-heritage.org.uk

The cemetery at Powerscourt in the Republic of Ireland includes cats, dogs and cows.

Index

Page numbers in italic refer to illustrations.